D0405014

LETHAL JUDGMENTS

This book is due on the last date stamped below.
Failure to return books on the date due may result
in assessment of overdue fees.

LANDMARK LAW CASES

&

AMERICAN SOCIETY

Peter Charles Hoffer
N. E. H. Hull
Series Editors

MELVIN I. UROFSKY

Lethal Judgments

Assisted Suicide and American Law

UNIVERSITY PRESS OF KANSAS

© 2000 by Melvin I. Urofsky

Published by the University Press of Kansas (Lawrence, Kansas
66049), which was organized by the Kansas Board of Regents and is
operated and funded by Emporia State University, Fort Hays State
University, Kansas State University, Pittsburg State University, the
University of Kansas, and Wichita State University

Library of Congress Cataloging-in-Publication Data

Urofsky, Melvin I.
    Lethal judgments : assisted suicide and American law / Melvin I.
Urofsky.
        p. cm. — (Landmark law cases & American society)
    Includes bibliographical references and index.
    ISBN 0-7006-1010-3 (cloth : alk. paper) — ISBN 0-7006-1011-1
(pbk. : alk. paper)
    1. Assisted suicide—Law and legislation—United States.
2. Euthanasia—Law and legislation—United States. 3. Right to
die—Law and legislation—United States. I. Title. II. Series.

KF3827.E87 U755 2000
344.73'04197—dc21   99-053549

British Library Cataloguing in Publication Data is available.

Printed in the United States of America

10 9 8 7 6 5 4 3 2 1

The paper used in this publication meets the minimum requirements of
the American National Standard for Permanence of Paper for Printed
Library Materials Z39.48-1984.

FOR LESLIE

WELCOME TO THE FAMILY

CONTENTS

Lethal Judgments, Melvin Urofsky's second contribution to this series, is another welcome addition. In it he guides us through the tangled web of medical, social, and legal issues surrounding *Washington v. Glucksburg* and *Quill v. Vacco,* the two physician-assisted suicide cases the U.S. Supreme Court decided in 1997. As topical and dramatic as these cases are, they represent, as the author reminds us, "only the beginning" of the legal struggle to define a patient's right to die. Medical technology has become so advanced and the elderly members of our society so numerous that an issue that a century ago was no more than a distant cloud now fills the sky.

Urofsky deftly and intelligibly dissects the medical questions in these cases, differentiating between discontinuation of medical treatment, for example, unplugging the machines that keep a terminally ill or brain-dead patient alive; assisted suicide, in which the physician provides the means for a chronically ill patient, or one facing a painful death, to commit suicide; and active euthanasia, in which the doctor engages in a mercy killing of a patient who wishes to dies but is physically or psychologically unable to perform suicide. In the cases fitting the first fact pattern, courts and legislatures in all of the states have allowed physicians to terminate support systems and treatments. In the second type of case, only the state of Oregon has legalized assisted suicide, but debates over the procedure continue in other states. No state has legalized mercy killing. Many experts fear that insurance companies or families burdened with the escalating costs of caring for the chronically ill would abuse the opportunity. In individual cases, panels of theologians, philosophers, doctors, and jurists have reached widely divergent conclusions.

Urofsky's account sensitively and sympathetically probes the social and religious context of these arguments, enabling his readers to see both sides of the dispute. In the process, he links the cases to larger demographic and technological changes in our world. Modern medicine can prolong the lives of those with chronic pain and crippling disability for months and years. Although the Oregon experiment with legalization of assisted suicide has proved that most people wish to wait until the very end to exercise their legal privilege of assisted suicide, the number of people finding themselves in such straits grows every day.

One would think that the legislative arena was the place to sort out this mix of social and medical puzzles, for legislatures are the place where crimes are defined and medical policies established. Yet we live in an age of "rights" created and defended in the courts. The right to die in a place and manner of one's own choosing has been added to this list, but it raises for the courts thorny questions of human liberty and individual privacy, on the one hand, and the legitimate interests of the state in the health and welfare of its citizens, on the other. In his final chapters, Urofsky focuses on the two leading cases, from New York and Washington, exploring the briefs of counsel and "friends of the court" and the opinions of the judges. The result is a compelling account of physician-assisted suicide and the courts.

ACKNOWLEDGMENTS

There are many people who helped to make this book possible. During the time I was writing I had the benefit of wonderful students in a seminar I was teaching at the University of Richmond Law School on "Death, Dying and the Law." Hardin Lee Barton, Susan Bland, Caroline Browder, David Clements, Joy Draper, Lisa Greenfield, Catherine Indelicato, Surina Jossan, John Sung-Hyun Jung, Jeffrey King, Lisa Langendorfer, Kirsten Mackey, Katherine Mae Salt, David Vogt, Karen Welch, and Janet Westbrook undertook their various assignments with a real spirit of adventurousness, and their questions and insights helped me refine some of the ideas in this book.

Several doctors spoke with me during the course of research and writing on this book, including Frederick R. Weiss of Santa Ana, California, and William Regelson at the Medical College of Virginia. I also had the pleasure of meeting with a faculty seminar at the Medical School of Eastern Carolina University, and their comments on palliative care and the political problems of legalizing assisted suicide proved very helpful.

John Paul Jones and Michael Wolf of the University of Richmond Law School, Jill Norgren and Philippa Strum of the City University of New York, and Philip Urofsky of the Justice Department read an early draft of sections of this book that appeared as a law review article. Robert Urofsky took time from his own work as a graduate student at the University of Virginia to serve as a research assistant, and showed me how much there is available on the Web. He and Leslie Rezac read and commented on the penultimate draft of the manuscript. By the time this book appears, Leslie will have married Robert and joined our family. This book is dedicated to her by way of welcome.

Parts of chapters 1 and 2 originally appeared in a slightly different form in an earlier book of mine, *Letting Go: Death, Dying, and the Law* (1991), while chapters 6 and 7 originally appeared in an article in the *University of Richmond Law Review* (1998).

My thanks to Peter Hoffer and Natalie Hull for inviting me to add another title to this series. Finally, it is always a pleasure to work with Michael Briggs and his staff at the University Press of Kansas. Special thanks to production editor Rebecca Knight Giusti, copy editor Carol A. Kennedy, and designer Rich Hendel. They have learned the fine art of helping a writer produce a book with minimal stress on both.

Prologue: Jane Roe et al.

We know them only as "Jane Roe," "John Doe," and "James Poe," their true identities hidden by the language of a legal system committed to protecting the privacy of ordinary people. Nor do we know very much about them. Jane Roe had been a pediatrician, a professional woman, and through her career she had cared for thousands of children. Retired and sixty-nine years old, she had breast cancer that had spread throughout her skeleton and left her in constant pain. John Doe had been an artist. We do not know in what medium he worked, but although only forty-four years old, he could work no longer. He had contracted AIDS, and that in turn had led to a degenerative eye disease; it had already cost him more than 70 percent of his vision and would soon lead to total blindness. James Poe had been a sales representative, and we might surmise that he had been a heavy smoker, since he now suffered from emphysema. Sixty-nine years old, he could breathe only with the aid of an oxygen tank, and even then he felt a constant sense of suffocation, for which he took morphine regularly to ease the panic attacks.

We do not know if they knew each other, but they all had one thing in common—they wanted to die and end their suffering, and they wanted a doctor to help them out of this world. They found a group willing to help them, Compassion in Dying, but the laws of the State of Washington prohibited physician-assisted suicide. They could not understand the rationale of a law that mandated their continued suffering. After all, couldn't they end their lives if they wished to do so? And why should they have to resort to a gun or to poison when doctors possessed the means by which they could exit this world peacefully and without pain? It seemed to them that their rights, whatever those rights might be—privacy, bodily autonomy, perhaps even just a simple right to die—had been violated, and like countless Americans over the years, they went to court to demand that the state stop transgressing on their constitutionally protected rights.

Jane Roe, John Doe, and James Poe, along with Compassion in Dying and several sympathetic doctors, began a lawsuit on the West Coast, arguing that their personal rights under the Fourteenth Amendment to the Constitution had been violated by the State of Washington statute. On the East Coast, another group of patients and doctors filed a similar suit. Jane Roe and John Doe died before their case came to court, and James Poe soon thereafter, but the federal courts, right on up to the Supreme Court of the United States, heard their arguments. This book is about those cases, about the law surrounding their claims, and about the moral debate over physician-assisted suicide.

The various cases dealt with the same question: Do the rights protected by the Constitution include assistance from a physician or other person should one wish to commit suicide? In the majority opinion in the Supreme Court, the legal issues involved appeared easy to answer, and as we shall see, Chief Justice William H. Rehnquist treated the matter as a simple one. In fact, the issue was—and is—far from simple, and there is little doubt that assisted suicide will, in the not too distant future, be back before the high court again.

If we were to treat assisted suicide simply as a legal question, we would miss the real importance of this issue. The debate over assisted suicide, like all momentous questions in American history, is being argued in the courts. Americans, as Alexis de Tocqueville noted over a century and a half ago, always turn major social and political debates into judicial controversies. Landmark court cases, like the desegregation ruling in *Brown v. Board of Education* (1954) or the abortion decision in *Roe v. Wade* (1973), are important, but they do not take place in a vacuum. In the debate over assisted suicide, theologians and ethicists, rabbis, ministers, and priests, advocates for various interest groups, legislators and lobbyists, prosecutors and juries, as well as judges, are all caught up in a controversy that has fierce moral, ethical, and social connotations.

In some ways legal questions are relatively easy to answer. The purpose of the law is to ensure certainty, and whether by common law or by statute, once the facts are ascertained, then rules can be developed to guide people in the future. In contract law, for example, when one party promises to do something, the law expects that person to perform what has been promised. If, for example, A promises to sell a horse to B for $100, and then delivers a mule, A has not kept his promise; he has "breached" the contract. Once a court has determined the facts, that it was indeed a horse that had been promised but a mule delivered, then there are legal rules by which B can be compensated for any loss suffered as a result of the breach.

The law recognizes that not all promises can be kept, and in some instances it may be advantageous to a party not to fulfill the obligation. The law takes these considerations into account in the remedy that is provided to the party suffering from the breach. In terms of morality or social and economic considerations, there is very little debate. Our society and economy rely upon parties performing what they have promised to do. From an ethical point of view, a promise made is a promise that should be kept, and if it is not kept, then the aggrieved party should be made as whole as possible. There is no large interest group or philosophical school that argues that contracts should not be fulfilled, that there should be no penalties incurred by a breach.

But when we deal with questions of death, dying, and the law, and especially with assisted suicide, the social and ethical voices in the debate are many, and there is no unanimity. The voices range from those who believe in the full autonomy of the individual to those who argue that since only God can give life, then only God may end it. Within the medical profession, a group most familiar with death and dying, there are enormous divisions of opinion. The professional societies, like the American Medical Association, condemn assisted suicide, but polls of practicing physicians indicate a majority favor it.

Those of us who teach constitutional and legal history constantly remind our students that law is a reflection of society, that one cannot understand the development of the law or of constitutional doctrine except if one sees it in the larger context of social, economic, political, and cultural development. This is not a new idea. One hundred years ago Oliver Wendell Holmes, Roscoe Pound, Ernst Freund, and Louis Brandeis called for a "sociological jurisprudence," in which judges and lawyers took into account the rapid changes in society resulting from the industrialization of America.

Today most scholars agree that law can be understood only within the larger social context, and there is no subject in which this lesson can be learned more dramatically than in the debate over assisted suicide and the connected question of the so-called right to die. If we look only at the cases, we will not even learn the law, because of the fractured nature of the opinions. We must look at the changes that have taken place in the United States in the last few decades that have created a climate in which death, once a taboo subject, is debated in books, magazines, and newspapers, on radio and television talk shows, and in legislatures and referenda. Forty years ago if a person was in a bad accident or suffered from a serious illness, medicine could do little. Now we have organ transplants, open-heart surgery, miracle drugs, and machines that can keep the body functioning even when the brain is dead. It is impossible to imagine a scenario such as Dr. Jack Kevorkian's hooking up his "mercy machine" in the back of a beat-up Volkswagen bus except in an America of the 1990s.

The AIDS epidemic, the aging of America, the growing cost of medicine, a culture that values youth and beauty rather than age and wisdom, the advent of managed care, the debate over abortion, the emphasis on individual rights and autonomy—all these have played and continue to play a role in the debate. To understand *Compassion in Dying v. Washington* and *Quill v. Vacco,* we have to understand the cultural and ethical climate in which these cases arose, as well as the laws that they challenged. For the larger context in which these issues are being played out

4   { *Lethal Judgments* }

is that of individual liberties, the question of how much autonomy we are willing to grant to the individual balanced against the needs or demands of the community.

Although this book is based around the assisted suicide cases that the Supreme Court decided in 1997, it deals with a large variety of issues that must be examined if one is to understand the importance of the cases. As a result, the narrative is less chronological in nature than in some other case studies, because the issues are not themselves time-bound. We first look at the debate over suicide, a question that goes back to the Greeks and the Old Testament. While there is a great deal of Anglo-American law on suicide, the reader needs to keep in mind that in the end, most of the debate over suicide, and over assisted suicide, is not over legal questions but over what advocates see as moral questions. To one person, a sick and suffering woman taking an overdose of drugs is exercising her God-given right to control her own life; to another, it is an affront to the God who gave life. A doctor helping a terminally ill cancer patient leave this world at his own time is, to some people, an angel of mercy; to others, she is a cold-blooded murderer.

But death is not so simple as the extremists on either side would portray, and in the United States we have had not one but a number of debates over the years on what constitutes a "good death," on what options a person may exercise under the liberty interests protected in the Fourteenth Amendment, on just how far courts should be involved in these decisions. These issues are also examined, and they provide the context in which we can better understand what the Supreme Court decided.

Finally, unlike some of the great cases of the past, the assisted suicide cases are not the judiciary's last words on the subject, but only the beginning. This is not a moot issue, in which the legal elements have been decided once and for all. What the Court said in *Compassion in Dying* was that given the facts as they now stand, it declined to substitute its judgment for that of the state legislature, but should these facts materially change, should the state make end-of-life choices too narrow, then the Court would revisit the issue.

This book, then, is about an ongoing debate. The Jane Roes and John Does in these cases, even if we do not know their real names, are nonetheless very real persons, and they could easily be an aunt or an uncle, a parent or a spouse or a child. It could even be you.

CHAPTER I

Suicide

We must start with the subject of suicide itself, what the law says about it, and how modern ethicists as well as the major religions view the act of self-murder. To many people, it is one thing for a terminally ill person who is suffering great pain and loss of dignity to request that life support be withdrawn; the resulting death is, in many ways, "natural," even a "blessing." But they do not understand how someone who is not terminally ill, who may have months—perhaps even years—of life left to live, can deliberately elect death.

Suicide puzzles and scares people; life, after all, is so precious, how can anyone not at death's door wish to open and pass through that portal? As Shakespeare wrote: "Then is it sin/ To rush into the secret house of death/ Ere death dare come to us?" Western religions and western law have both frowned on suicide for centuries, yet it now appears that the miracles of medical technology that can prolong life have also triggered a new debate: Is it acceptable to allow a person to choose death, and if so, how may it be done, and who, if anyone, may assist?

Although some ancient Greek philosophies supported suicide, in general the populace viewed taking one's own life as unnatural. In Athenian law the hand that committed the suicide would be cut off and buried apart from the rest of the body, which itself would be denied normal funeral rites. Even the most famous suicide of the ancient world, Socrates, denounced the practice, and justified only suicides demanded by the gods. In his own case, he declared that since the city-state embodied divine will, the command of the Athenian authorities must be obeyed. Other Greek writers also acknowledged the legitimacy of suicide under limited circumstances.

The Romans for the most part accepted the idea of suicide. As Seneca wrote, "Just as I shall select my ship when I am about to go on a voyage, or my house when I propose to take a residence, so I shall choose my death when I am about to depart from life." Roman law never included any general prohibition of suicide. There were, however, some special provisions. If a person committed suicide to avoid forfeiture of property for a crime, the property would still be forfeit. A soldier could be punished for attempted suicide, on the ground that this constituted a desertion of duty, itself a crime against the state.

Prohibitions against suicide made their way into canon law beginning with St. Augustine, who in *The City of God,* written in the early fifth century, condemned self-murder as "a detestable and damnable wickedness." Augustine interpreted a number of different biblical sources to "prove" that God had forbidden suicide.

Since in the Middle Ages secular authorities recognized canon law as binding in any area related to church teaching, the various pronouncements of the Catholic Church regarding self-murder quickly crowded out earlier pagan acceptance of suicide. The edicts of the Council of Orleans in 533 implied that suicide was worse than any other crime, and the Council of Braga in 563 denied to suicides normal funeral rites, such as the Eucharist and the singing of psalms. In England, the Council of Hereford in 673 adopted canon law, and King Edgar in 967 specifically affirmed the denial of burial rites; in 1284, the Synod of Nîmes ruled that suicides could not be interred in holy ground. St. Thomas Aquinas, the greatest of the medieval scholastics, reflected the view of the church that killing oneself was one of the few sins that guaranteed everlasting damnation in hell. "Whoever takes his own life, sins against God," Aquinas wrote, "for it belongs to God alone to pronounce sentence of life and death." Dante, in *The Inferno,* put suicides in the seventh circle of hell, lower than murderers and heretics.

8   { *Lethal Judgments* }

The growth of the common law (i.e., judge-made law) in England saw the canonical rules, including the practice of dishonoring the corpse, absorbed and strengthened. An early seventeenth-century writer noted that the suicide's body "is drawn by a horse to the place of punishment and shame, where he is hanged on a gibbet, and none may take the body down but by the authority of a magistrate." A century and a half later Blackstone wrote that suicides would be buried at a crossroads, with a stake driven through the heart and a stone placed over the face. (Other cultures that considered suicide a taboo also treated the body in a manner designed to keep it from contaminating the tribe. Alabama Indians, for example, threw the corpse into a river, while people in Dahomey carried the body out where it would be food for carrion-eaters.)

The last known crossroads burial of a suicide in England took place in 1823, after which Parliament passed a law calling for private burial in a churchyard, but at night and without religious rites. In 1882 an amendment allowed daytime internment, although still without the Church of England ritual. Only a verdict by a coroner's jury that the deceased had been mentally unbalanced, and therefore not responsible for his or her actions, would allow a normal church burial to proceed.

The early settlers of New England brought with them both legal and religious proscriptions against suicide. In 1660 the Massachusetts General Court, in "bear[ing] testimony against such wicked and unnatural practices," ruled that self-murderers "shall be denied the privilege of being buried in the common burying place of Christians, but shall be buried in some common highway where the selectmen of the town ... shall appoint, and a cartload of stones laid upon the grave, as a brand of infamy, and as a warning to others to beware of the like damnable practices." Although the practice fell into disuse, the statute itself was not repealed until 1823. The United States, however, did not adopt English common law crimes, so suicide constituted a criminal act only in those states that specifically made it so by statute.

What the law thinks is of little concern to the successful self-murderer, who is beyond the reach of the magistrate. But what of those who fail in their attempts, who do not take sufficient poison or sedatives, whose aim is off, whose booby traps fail to work? In many states where suicide is not a crime, attempted suicide is, and the person who wakes up after a failed attempt may face criminal prosecution.

These statutes also trace back to English common law. The courts reasoned that every attempt to commit a crime is punishable; suicide is a crime, and therefore attempted suicide may be punished. But how did suicide itself get to be a crime? Self-murder violated canon law, but the church, while condemning it as mortal sin, only called for a denial of burial rites. Around the tenth century King Edgar ruled that a suicide's property would be forfeit to his feudal lord; somewhat later the rule changed so that a suicide's estate would be forfeit to the Crown. In order to justify this change, the royal courts noted that every felon forfeited his goods to the king; by making suicide a felony, they could apply the general rule to suicide as well.

In *Hales v. Petit* (1562), one of the first cases to equate suicide with other felonies, the court condemned suicide as a criminal act, an offense against nature, against God, and against the king. Blackstone denounced suicide as "a double offence: one spiritual, in evading the prerogative of the Almighty, and rushing into his immediate presence uncalled for; the other temporal, against the king, who hath an interest in the preservation of all his subjects."

The first known case involving the legal punishment of attempted suicide dates to 1854, in which the learned judges held the criminality of attempted suicide a self-evident truth. Within a few years other decisions confirmed the rule, and what began as a moral indictment, enlarged by the monarch's greed for property, became an accepted rule of common law—suicide constituted a felony, and while the successful felon escaped the law's punishment, the failed suicide would certainly stand in the dock.

The idiocy of this rule, which existed both in England and in America, seems obvious. As Glanville Williams wrote:

Quite apart from the general debate on the ethics of suicide, the punishment of attempted suicide has to meet the twin objection that it is cruel and inefficacious. The prime fact about suicide is that legal sanctions cannot stop it. No country has ever succeeded in repressing suicide by this method; the threat of punishment for attempted suicide can only make the offender more likely, if anything, to make sure of succeeding at the first attempt. But for most persons the threat will have no effect one way or the other, because people who are bent on throwing their lives away are not likely to consider the possibility of punishment on failure.

Not until the Suicide Act of 1961 did Her Majesty's Government finally stop making suicide or its attempt a crime.

Other countries had taken that step long before. The writings of the eighteenth-century criminologist Beccaria led to France's decriminalizing of attempted suicide shortly after the French Revolution, and most other countries on the Continent followed suit in the early nineteenth century. Even when Germany, Italy, and Russia fell under the rule of totalitarian governments in the twentieth century and introduced strict population policies, they did not reenact criminal laws regarding suicide or its attempt.

In the United States today, even in those few jurisdictions where statutes still make attempted suicide a crime, there are no prosecutions. At worst, a failed attempt may lead to mandated therapy or perhaps incarceration in a mental hospital. The criminal stigma has for the most part disappeared, although most religions and many people still condemn self-murder as morally wrong.

Following the Enlightenment, the Western world became less dominated by religious thought, and the absolute moral condemnation against suicide partially dissipated. Even as English judges criminalized suicide, philosophers began suggesting that not all self-murders are bad or even immoral and that some might be defended on both rational and moral grounds.

In 1561 Thomas More allowed for suicide in his *Utopia*. A century later John Donne, in *Biathanatos* (1647), argued that contrary to classical Christian teachings, the taking of one's life is not incompatible with the laws of nature, of reason, or of God. Perhaps the most famous of the early justifications is David Hume's essay *On Suicide* (1777), in which he reasoned that a suicide is wrong only if it offends God, one's neighbor, or one's self, but such consequences are not always the case. Hume believed that God had given mankind free will and that this included the freedom to take one's own life, especially if one's life had become unbearable. "That suicide may often be consistent with interests and with duty to *ourselves*," Hume wrote, "no one can question, who allows that age, sickness, or misfortune may render life a burden, and make it worse even than annihilation." Other Enlightenment writers, including Voltaire, Rousseau, Montesquieu, and d'Halbach, endorsed Hume's argument.

The large number of volumes on library shelves dealing with suicide from ethical, sociological, psychological, religious, and metaphysical viewpoints shows conclusively that it is far from a moot issue today. For some people, taking one's life, no matter what the circumstances, is wrong, and even if not in violation of secular law is an affront to God's law. For others, one's life is one's own, and each person must determine whether it is worth living. To tie the notion of suicide to contemporary law, the issue must be cast not in religious terms but in the framework of personal autonomy, but the questions are far more complex than the simplistic and often heard "Whose life is it anyway?"

Two of the leading students of biomedical ethics, Tom Beauchamp and James Childress, have suggested certain criteria for determining whether or not a particular suicide is moral. They list three principles: human worth, utility, and autonomy; the last is particularly apposite when it comes to the law.

The issue of human worth, referred to by some as the "sanctity of human life," raises the question of whether life is so intrinsically valuable that its self-destruction is an act of murder and therefore wrong. The great humanitarian Albert Schweitzer wrote: "The ethics of respect for life does not recognize any relative ethics. It admits as good only the preservation and advancement of life. All destruction and harming of life, no matter what the circumstances under which this may occur, it designates as evil." On the other side is the argument that existence must be meaningful, that the quality of a life is important, and that if that quality is eroded, through debilitating illness or great despair, then life no longer has any worth.

Although suicide is intensely personal, it affects other people in a variety of ways. Beauchamp and Childress argue that would-be suicides must look beyond their own reasons for ending life and see how great a harm, if any, this act would cause other people. Without a family or obligations to others, a utilitarian calculus has no negative items to balance the desire to end pain, suffering, or any other condition the person finds intolerable. If, on the other hand, there is a dependent family or if the person has talents the absence of which would deprive society, then Beauchamp and Childress would put this into the balance against suicide.

There are, of course, many other factors that could enter the calculations, such as whether the stigma of suicide might be injurious to relatives, especially children. The Beauchamp-Childress proposal is not meant to be exclusive, but merely to point out that various considerations must be taken into account. In its starkest form, the "utilitarian demand [is] that the greatest possible amount of value or at least the smallest amount of disvalue be brought about by the person's actions."

A similar view is propounded by Richard Momeyer, who sees suicide as an individual right. He argues that, first, each person's life belongs to that person alone, and like other property, may be disposed as the owner pleases. Second, when a competent person makes such a decision, respect for individual autonomy requires the same respect as is given to other choices that one makes regarding one's life. Finally, making a decision about how one wishes to die should be considered as a fundamental right, as important to an individual as the rights of property or speech.

But Momeyer, like most other advocates of suicide, does not see it as an unlimited right, and does not surround it with the type of calculus suggested by Beauchamp and Childress. For Momeyer, the right to kill oneself is hedged by the need to serve human dignity. Thus a person jilted by a lover is not acting with dignity when he wants to jump off a bridge; a woman suffering from cancer who can no longer lead a meaningful existence is acting to preserve her dignity when she takes a lethal dose of barbiturates.

The strongest argument in favor of allowing individual discretion is that of autonomy, which has become a major issue in modern law. The Supreme Court, even while downplaying privacy, has emphasized the right of personal autonomy, which it finds embedded in the liberty interests protected by the Fourteenth Amendment. Under this line of reasoning, individuals have, within very broad parameters, the right to govern their own lives and to decide, if competent, when to end their lives by refusing continued medical care. If one truly believes in the autonomy of each individual, it would be, according to Beauchamp and Childress, "a showing of disrespect to deny autonomous persons the right to commit suicide when, in their considered judgment, they ought to do so."

The decision is individual, and former Chief Justice Warren Burger, while still a circuit court judge, pointed out that it is the individual, and not the society, that determines what is best for himself or herself:

> Mr. Justice Brandeis, whose views have inspired much of the "right to be let alone" philosophy, said: "The makers of our Constitution . . . sought to protect Americans in their beliefs, their thoughts, their emotions, and their sensations. They conferred, as against the Government, the right to be let alone—the most comprehensive of rights and the right most valued by civilized man." Nothing in this utterance suggests that Justice Brandeis thought an individual possessed these rights only as to sensible beliefs, valid thoughts, reasonable emotions, or well-founded sensations. I suggest he intended

to include a great many foolish, unreasonable, and even absurd ideas which do not conform.

Each of these three notions, human worth, utility, and above all autonomy, is a powerful argument, and should be binding upon all those who, for whatever reason, would seek to interfere. As Beauchamp and Childress note: "If a suicide were genuinely autonomous and there were no powerful utilitarian reasons or reasons of human worth and dignity standing in the way, then we ought to allow the person to commit suicide, because we would otherwise be violating the person's autonomy. . . . The morality of suicide cannot be determined in abstraction from the facts of a person's own situation."

Obviously there are limits on autonomy, and no one suggests that it should mean unbridled self-interest. For example, if a person decided it was in his best interest to get a lot of money by robbing a bank, that would be unacceptable, because other individuals as well as society would lose. But in talking about suicide, ethicists who support autonomy are concerned only with the individual and others to whom he or she relates within a relatively close circle. Most advocates of suicide as an individual right concede that it is not an unlimited right and that it should be exercised under certain constraints. Despite Cassandra-like warnings from opponents, defenders of individual autonomy do not propose drive-through suicide clinics, a sort of "McDeath," where one can get a poison pill along with a vanilla shake and french fries.

Because suicide is so final a decision, some people question whether it can be rational. Even if one concedes that a person has a "right" to commit suicide, is it possible to choose to end one's life through a thoughtful and logical process? Alan Johnson, one of the leaders of the Hemlock Society, believes that suicide can be a rational choice, and at the heart of his argument are the notions of personal dignity and quality of life. People can intelligently arrive at the conclusion that under the circumstances, they would rather die than continue living.

He relates the story of his stepmother, who told him, *"I do not choose to die in diapers!"* A woman who had been a volunteer ambulance nurse in World War I and who headed a major unit at the San Diego Naval Hospital in the next war, she loved life and was not afraid of death, but only of a dying process in which she would lose control of her mind and body and become a burden to others. Unfortunately, she did suffer enormously, both physically and psychologically, and no one could help her. For Johnson, her wish to die was perfectly rational, far more rational than society's unwillingness to allow her to go out as she wanted. As in so many areas of contemporary debate, the key issue is *who decides.* For proponents of suicide, that decision must be solely that of the individual.

———

The debate, however, is not one-sided. Many of the opponents of suicide in general and of assisted suicide in particular base their objections on religious grounds, while some prominent medical ethicists aver that there are other, and more important, considerations than personal autonomy.

The opponents deny that there is any right to die in general, and to commit suicide in particular. Victor Rosenblum and Clarke Forsythe are among the strongest opponents of a so-called right to die. They take the view that Western legal and civil traditions had good reasons to condemn suicide, since suicide takes place most often among society's most vulnerable members—the sick, the aged, the infirm, the mentally incompetent. At the most, they are willing to concede a right not to accept medication or undergo surgery, even if the proposed treatment might increase life span. Although people might disagree about the utility of the medical treatment, death would result from the disease, and not from a willful act. In this Rosenblum and Forsythe tacitly endorse a passive euthanasia, but strongly reject any active steps to shorten one's life. Life is too precious, too sacred, they argue, to allow one to just throw it away.

Daniel Callahan of the Hastings Institute rejects what he considers the wrong-headed argument about individual autonomy. We live in a society, Callahan notes, and as such the interests of the group take precedence over the wishes of the individual. Suicide undermines social obligations and weakens the community, which has its own rights, one of which is to outlaw life-threatening activities. Callahan is part of a larger communitarian movement that believes that many of the ills of modern society have arisen from an emphasis on, indeed an obsession about, individualism; in their haste to "be themselves," people have forgotten their obligations to others. As Mona Charen wrote, "We're a nation drunk on rights, and always willing to have one more for the road. . . . What suicide proponents don't understand is that no individual is completely independent. We need each other."

The most potent arguments against suicide are those grounded in morality. While the major Western religions do not object to the voluntary termination of medical treatment, especially heroic measures, for the terminally ill, they all draw the line at suicide.

A strict reading of Jewish law and tradition, at least as interpreted by contemporary Orthodox scholars, suggests that one must not do anything to hasten death and must do everything possible to prolong life. But there is no positive obligation to delay natural death, and this permits the removal of any artificial hindrance to dying. Jewish doctors are permitted, by this interpretation, to withhold mechanical devices and medication that would delay a natural death, but may not withdraw food and water, even if it must be administered through tubes.

Traditional Jewish law forbids suicide, and although there is no specific biblical prohibition against it, a passage in Genesis 9:5, "surely your blood of your lives will I require," has been construed to mean that only God may take one's life. The Jewish Bible mentions only four suicides, and while none of these is condemned, either in the sacred text itself or in the various rabbinical commentaries, they are seen as the results of great stress. The Talmud, in fact, distinguishes between suicide by one of sound mind *(la-da'at)* and by one of unsound mind *(she-lo la-da'at)*. Throughout the ages it appears that rabbis have sought even the slightest evidence of mental strain so as to place the suicide in the latter category and therefore not to be held responsible.

Catholicism, perhaps more than any other religion, opposes active euthanasia in any form. The early church interpreted the gospels' accounts of Jesus healing the sick and the parable of the Good Samaritan (Luke 10:25–37) to mean that one should help the sick and wounded. Instead of viewing the diseased and the elderly as burdens that society could eliminate, the church viewed illness as a form of suffering that purifies the victims and enobles those who help them. Early church leaders gradually began to condemn any activity that destroyed life, such as abortion, infanticide, exposure, or suicide. Saint Augustine declared that God's command against killing others also prohibited self-destruction. As to ending one's own life because of great pain or suffering, or helping others to end theirs, Augustine saw suffering as a necessary purification before a person could enter the kingdom of heaven. "The tides of trouble will test, purify, and improve the good, but beat, crush, and wash away the wicked."

While church doctrine still condemns suicide, the technology of modern medicine and the problems it has created have also caused some tensions between official dogma and the realities of the world. Typical of the traditional attitude is the comment by J. P. Kenney that "there is a certain unnaturalness associated with the desire to terminate one's life deliberately. . . . Moreover, ecclesiastical penalties imposed by Canon Law upon those guilty of violating the Fifth Commandment by suicide or homicide are no less applicable to cases where a 'mercy' motive could be alleged." Catholic doctrine considers suicide an "unlawful moral act," and the suicide is not given ecclesiastical burial unless he or she showed repentance before death. The only exception is the category of "indirect suicide," where a person is aware that certain actions may result in his or her death, but balances that by a greater good, for example, by deliberating steering one's car over a cliff in order to avoid a fatal crash with a school bus full of children.

More liberal Catholic thinkers, such as Daniel Maguire, have adopted a form of situation ethics, in which the person's actions should be judged within the context of the circumstances. Thus Daniel Maguire has declared that "the morality of terminating life, innocent or not, is an open question although it is widely treated as a closed one." This is, however, definitely a minority opinion, and official Catholic teaching still emphasizes the primacy and sacredness of life. Euthanasia in any form, including physician-assisted suicide, is forbidden.

In 1978, the *Linacre Quarterly,* the official journal of the National Federation of Catholic Physicians' Guilds, carried a widely quoted article by Dr. Russell L. McIntyre in which he declared that under no circumstances ought "euthanasia be considered as an alternative to care. We have no moral ground on which to stand, whatever, if we euthanize to avoid care." However, McIntyre went on to say that prolonging life beyond the moment when "the presence of God [is] being withdrawn" is also indefensible. Thus, in specific instances where a person is brain dead, in an irreversible coma, or in a persistent vegetative state, the physician should do nothing to prolong life. Using Charles Curran's terminology, Dr. McIntyre noted that when the "process of dying" has overtaken the "process of living," the physician should recognize this as God's will and not try to interfere.

The debate within the Catholic Church in the 1970s, as well as the fact that two of the major right to die cases in the United States involved Catholic patients, Karen Quinlan and Brother Joseph Fox, led to the issuance by the Sacred Congregation for the Doctrine of the Faith of a "Declaration on Euthanasia," approved by Pope John Paul II on May 5, 1980. Even before the declaration, John Paul and his predecessor, Pope Paul VI, had condemned euthanasia as incompatible with Catholic teaching. The Vatican Declaration reaffirmed the historic Catholic view regarding the value and sanctity of life as a gift from God. The statement also repeated the Catholic Church's traditional condemnation of suicide, an act it equated with murder and denounced as "a rejection of God's sovereignty and loving plan." While denouncing active euthanasia, the document acknowledged a right to die, not by suicide or at another's hands, "but to die peacefully with human and Christian dignity." The Declaration does, however, permit cessation and refusal of heroic measures and removal of artificial life support.

It would be impossible to detail the views of every Protestant faith, especially since many have no official doctrine on the subject, while those that emphasize congregational organization may leave the decision either to individual conscience or to local mores. Typical of the latter is the statement of John K. Martin of the Anglican Consultative Council. As far as he could tell, the Anglican Church had never adopted any statement on euthanasia, but a number of individual churches that belonged to the Anglican Communion had "expressed their mind on this matter, if not through their synods, then through research and the engagement of their Boards for Social Responsibility."

Similarly, not only are the Baptists split into several general associations, but each church is an independent unit. Probably most Baptists would subscribe to the statement of the General Association of General Baptists: "We believe life and death belong in the hands of God. . . . We oppose euthanasia, sometimes referred to as mercy killing. . . . We affirm the right of every person to die with dignity. We reject efforts made to prolong terminal illnesses merely because the technology is available to do so."

Although it is assumed that the Protestants, like the Catholics and Jews, proscribe suicide and active euthanasia, most Protestant denominations have no formal theological position. As a result, one finds prominent clerics and laypersons advocating suicide and even active euthanasia as within the traditions of their faiths. The Reverend Joseph Fletcher, for example, argued for legalized euthanasia on the grounds that suffering is purposeless, human personality is worth more than mere existence, and perhaps most important, the phrase "Blessed are the merciful, for they shall obtain mercy" is as important as "Thou shalt not kill." The then archbishop of Canterbury, in addressing the Royal Society of Medicine in 1976, denounced the idea that it is "Christian" to prolong life artificially just for the sake of doing so, and he quoted approvingly the nineteenth-century poet Arthur Clough, that "Thou should not kill, but needst not strive officiously to keep alive."

Paul D. Simmons of the Southern Baptist Seminary shocked many people when he argued that Christianity could approve of some types of suicide. Those who elect death by direct and voluntary means, he declared,

> may be seen as acting in the context of the Christian freedom to choose the terms under which they are to die. Suicide of this type is hardly to be regarded as a sin for which there is no forgiveness. On the contrary, such a decision may be based upon a commitment to the truth that "whether we live or whether we die, we are the Lord's" (Rom. 14:8).

In general, however, the various Protestant denominations do not offer any cohesive approach to euthanasia or suicide, and in practice leave the decision to the individual. A few groups have issued doctrinal statements; the governing body of the United Church of Christ, for example, recently affirmed the right of terminally ill people to commit suicide and of their relatives to end their lives for them. The recent rise in interest in the right to die has also led some social action committees to issue statements that, for the most part, oppose active euthanasia while affirming the right of each individual to die with dignity.

In essence, the religious view is that when death is nigh, it is neither sinful nor an obligation to delay the soul's departure. The removal of artificial life support, such as respirators, is not the true cause of death; rather the person dies from the underlying illness. Some religious leaders oppose even this position, arguing that life is so precious that one must do all that is humanly possible to keep even a faint spark alive. For the most part, the general view is that passive euthanasia through the removal of artificial life supports does not violate religious teaching.

Suicide, however, is nearly universally condemned by religious groups and by many communitarian-minded ethicists, and as a result we get a far more vehement argument when it comes to assisted suicide. But one also needs to recall the old Greek notion of a good death. Today in America that notion, seemingly out of usage for so long, is making a remarkable comeback.

CHAPTER 2

The Good Death in America

The term "euthanasia" is used frequently in his book, and figures prominently in the debates over the right to die and physician-assisted suicide. One side uses it as a term of idealism, referring to the original Greek word meaning the "good death" to which all of us aspire—peaceful, pain-free, surrounded by our loved ones. Opponents see it as a term of murder, killing those who are sick, infirm, or disabled, young and old alike, with or without their permission. In their view, the murderers are doctors who forsake their Hippocratic oath and play God with the lives of their patients.

Until relatively recently, euthanasia had little to do with doctors, but referred to the experience of the dying person. Doctors, according to the original code of ethics of the American Medical Association, had the obligation to comfort their patients and when possible to revive them. The state of medical knowledge in the mid-nineteenth century, however, led most doctors to believe they should let nature take its course. They might prescribe a cordial, probably an opium derivative, to ease the pain, and because they had ministered not only to the patient but to the family, they joined in the death watch and did what they could to comfort the living. Because nearly everyone died at home in those days, we have no data on just what doctors actually did, but the anecdotal evidence is that many doctors saw it as their duty to relieve the pain, even to the point of causing their patient's death. As one doctor told a public symposium in 1913, "Others have assumed the responsibility which I myself have taken in more than one case, of producing euthanasia."

Whether doctors acted on their own, or acceded to the wishes of the patient and family, is impossible to tell, but we can surmise that what we now call physician-assisted suicide took place in at least some instances. Doctors who could do little except relieve pain might well acquiesce to a patient's desire to end all suffering. In some ways, modern advocates of physician-assisted suicide want to return, not to the state of medical knowledge in the nineteenth century, but to a condition in which patients could look for a good death and expect help from the doctors whom they had known and trusted for years.

In the twentieth century medical knowledge and practice underwent an enormous expansion. By the end of the century this explosion had outpaced the ability of the public and perhaps some doctors to comprehend its magnitude. At the twenty-fifth reunion of the Columbia College class of 1961, one physician told his classmates that the material and most of the procedures he had learned in medical school in the early 1960s had long been obsolete, and that the half-life of new drugs and technology might be no more than four years. Doctors could now cure diseases that had once been considered incurable; old foes like measles, tuberculosis, and polio had practically been wiped out in the Western world; operations upon the brain and the heart, once considered a delusional fantasy, took place on a daily basis; organs could be transplanted from one person to another; machines using ultrasound and magnetic resonance could take pictures of the inside of the body far superior to the older X rays; and in some instances problems discovered in utero could be surgically corrected.

No one, especially a person who has benefited from this knowledge and technology, can complain about its beneficial effects. What might have been a fatal condition one hundred or even fifty years ago can now often be remedied by a common procedure, perhaps even on an outpatient basis. Infections that once took the lives of thousands are controlled by safe and inexpensive antibiotics. The life expectancy of the American people has increased dramatically in the last one hundred years; many people not only are living longer, but are living healthier lives as well.

There is, however, a downside to the wonders of modern medicine, a paradox of progress. Doctors cannot cure everyone, but in many cases they can keep that person "alive" far longer than might otherwise have been the case had they let nature take its course. There is still no "cure" for cancer, but radiation and chemotherapy, surgery and marrow transplants, can delay death, often for years. For the person whose cancer is in remission and whose daily life is relatively normal and pain-free, this is truly a blessing. But for some the therapy may be worse than the cure—endless treatments that are themselves painful, often resulting in a loss of bodily autonomy and control. For these people death may be a preferable option. For doctors the comfort and dignity of the patient has sometimes become secondary to the challenge of keeping him alive for as long as possible. Life, no matter how tortured and painful, has trumped death, no matter how desired.

The transformation of medical practice has not gone unchallenged. Throughout the past century there have been groups and individuals, some within the medical profession but most outside, who have argued against the "life at all costs" philosophy. They have demanded that the decision be returned to the patient and that the doctor follow the wishes of her patient, even if the technology exists to keep the patient alive. The law has always held the patient's wishes to be paramount, but in the medical culture of much of the twentieth century doctors became a law unto themselves. They would decide how to treat the patient; they would decide what would be in the best interest of the patient; and laypersons—including the patient—who could not possibly understand the technical issues involved, were not to question physician judgment. Not until the 1970s did this begin to change with the emergence of a patients' rights movement and the reemergence of the old common law rules on personal autonomy.

Even as the explosion in medical knowledge began, some groups fought to preserve what one nineteenth-century jurist termed "the natural right to a natural death." In some states advocates introduced bills to legalize euthanasia, and while these bills rarely got out of committee, they changed the definition of the term. Instead of referring to a patient's good or natural death, euthanasia now meant a doctor's actions to bring about death. Euthanasia began to be referred to in the popular press as homicide, and later efforts to make the good death possible only reinforced this image of doctors as murderers.

In 1938 a group of social reformers and doctors founded the Euthanasia Society of America, and they pointed to public opinion polls that seemed to support the notion of "mercy deaths." Unfortunately for the group's cause, newspapers at the time began carrying stories of Nazi programs in which German doctors put to death people who were mentally retarded, physically handicapped, elderly, or infirm. The eugenics movement, which had been very strong in the United States in the early part of the century, also suffered a setback, and euthanasia became wedded in the public mind with the Holocaust, in which the Hitler regime attempted not only to kill off Jews but to weed out other racially "unfit" groups, such as the Gypsies. Despite trying to explain the difference between the good death for the individual and Nazi racial policies, the Euthanasia Society lost membership and public support. By 1960 it had practically ceased to exist.

About that time, however, several developments in American society began to revive the notion not only of the good death, but also of patients' taking greater control over their fates. The Karen Ann Quinlan case, discussed in chapter 3, focused attention on a medical technology that could keep people breathing and therefore technically "alive" but could not restore them to life. Powerful new medicines, while sometimes curing people or slowing the ravages of disease, oftentimes merely stretched out the suffering of the dying process. The civil rights movement, and then the women's movement, also rekindled an interest in autonomy and led to a movement that would transfer power from doctors back to patients, especially in end-of-life treatments and decisions.

But to make these decisions, people had to start talking about death. Up until the end of the nineteenth century, people accepted death as natural. Without the tools of modern medicine, people succumbed rapidly to infectious disease, cancers, and the wounds of serious accidents. In a frontier society death was no stranger, and people dealt with it on a regular basis. Then with the development of powerful drugs, new surgical procedures, and better diets, people began living longer. If death itself could not be banished, talking about it could be, and social scientists in a variety of studies concluded that death had become a taboo subject.

One cannot say when that began to alter, but one might point to an event that if it did not trigger the change, certainly accelerated it. In 1957 Lael Wertenbaker published *Death of a Man,* her account of the last three months together with her husband before he took his life. Charles Wertenbaker, a writer, discovered he had an inoperable liver cancer. He decided to take pain killers, but determined that when the pain became unbearable or he could no longer live with dignity, he would kill himself. On the day after Christmas 1954, he told his wife that the time had come. "A gentleman should know when to take his leave."

Over the next decade medical and professional journals began carrying more articles on death and on training doctors, nurses, psychologists, and social workers to deal with it. Then starting in the late 1960s a veritable explosion of magazine articles and books appeared. According to one source, some 1,200 books in English on death and bereavement appeared between 1968 and 1973. On television, news shows as well as dramas suddenly began discussing death, and in 1972 the United States Senate Committee on Aging held hearings on "death with dignity."

The Quinlan trial did not trigger this avalanche; quite the opposite. The public's attention had already been focused by such works as Elisabeth Kübler-Ross's *On Death and Dying* (1969) and television movies such as *Brian's Song* (1970), about the death of Chicago Bears running back Brian Piccolo. Colleges and even public schools began offering courses on death and dying, on bereavement and grief. By the time the Quinlan case hit the headlines, the American public had already spent a decade thinking about death and especially how one might die with dignity. From a cultural rather than a legal standpoint, the Quinlan case focused that concern and brought it out even more into the open.

The Quinlan episode, and books like the posthumous memoir of journalist Stewart Alsop, who died after two years of treatment for leukemia, brought home the fact that death had ceased to be a single event and had become a long-term affair. Americans did not seem to fear death as much as they dreaded a long, drawn-out dying. In what is surely one of the most terrifying statistics of the 1970s, three-fourths of Americans spent an average of eighty days of the last year of life in a hospital bed or nursing home, often hooked up continuously to bottles of liquids and nutrients or life-support machines. The good death had turned into a nightmare of dying.

The very definition of death and of dying had changed. Once it had been simple—a person stopped breathing, or her heart stopped. Modern technology has rendered these definitions all but obsolete, with machines that will breathe for a person or even keep the heart beating. In 1968 a committee at the Harvard Medical School recommended that "brain death," the cessation of all brain functions, become the accepted medical definition of death. The Harvard criterion is sometimes referred to as "whole brain death," the state in which all parts of the brain have ceased to function and which would appear on an EEG monitor as a flat line.

Some doctors and ethicists, however, have suggested a "higher brain activity" test, referring to that part of the brain that controls cognitive function. Death in their view should be defined as the point when a person become physiologically incapable of cognitive activity. By the use of this test persons who are in a persistent vegetative state, who have no signs of cognitive activity but whose autonomous functions continue, could be declared dead. Most doctors and hospitals have refused to accept this test, and as long as there is any pattern on an EEG monitor, death is not declared.

It is little wonder that, given a political climate in which blacks, women, and other groups sought to take control of their lives and to claim rights they believed due to them, a "patients' rights" movement began as well. The notion of the doctor as a god, someone who knew best and whose judgment should not be questioned, receded as patients began demanding not only information about their illnesses and proposed treatment, but a voice in deciding whether to accept treatment. Like other establishment institutions, the medical profession slipped in public esteem, and opinion polls indicated that people no longer viewed physicians as infallible gods. The women's movement, which proclaimed that the personal is the political, attacked what it saw as the male-chauvinist basis of much modern medicine, especially in the area of obstetrics and gynecology, at the time overwhelmingly populated by male practitioners. In books such as *Our Bodies, Ourselves* (1973), women sought to retake control of their health decisions from the professionals.

This movement for personal control would, as we shall see in the next chapter, play itself out in the courts, but well before the litigation one could see evidence of the trend. The connection between the idea of a good death and that of a right to die might not always be well articulated, but people understood that if they wanted a death with dignity they would have to demand it as a right. In the early 1970s, again before the Quinlan case, 62 percent of Americans agreed that a terminally ill patient should have the right to refuse life-prolonging treatment.

———

In the 1970s and 1980s the media began to carry stories about so-called "mercy killings," people who acted to put a beloved friend or relative out of their suffering. One of the most famous of the cases, that of 75-year-old Roswell Gilbert, took place in 1985.

Roswell and Emily Gilbert had been married for fifty-one years, and no one questioned the retired electronics engineer's deep devotion to his 73-year-old wife. Throughout their married life he had catered to her every whim; the two were inseparable, and he used to say that they fit together like spoons. In 1978 they bought a condominium in Florida, and then what should have been golden years turned to sorrow. Emily's mental state gradually deteriorated from Alzheimer's disease; in addition, she suffered from osteoporosis, a bone disease that caused her much pain. Roswell became her caretaker as well as her husband, brushing her hair and teeth for her. Since he still had a small business as a consulting engineer, he took elaborate precautions never to leave her alone for more than a day.

The couple's only daughter, Martha Gilbert Moran, suspected that her mother had Alzheimer's as early as 1982, but her father refused to confirm it, trying to protect her from the knowledge. The following year Martha took her mother out, "and it was like taking a three-year-old to lunch. She couldn't even read the menu. She ordered tuna salad but didn't eat it. I took Mother to the ladies' room, and she wouldn't come out. I walked in to find her looking in the mirror vacantly. Later that afternoon she said that she hadn't seen me in over ten years."

On March 4, 1985, Ros Gilbert, a gun collector, put a single bullet into a 9mm Luger decorated with an American eagle. He came out of the bedroom and walked up behind Emily, and shot her through the temple. He felt her heart, which was still beating faintly, so he went back into the bedroom, reloaded the pistol, and shot her again. This time she died.

He walked out of the apartment into the hall and met their neighbor, Elizabeth Phillips. "Libby," he told her, "I just shot Emily." Mrs. Phillips ran to get her husband, a doctor, but nothing could be done for the woman. Roswell Gilbert then called the police, and when they arrived, reportedly told them that he was an engineer, and he had come up with a solution to the problem. The district attorney brought charges of first-degree murder against Gilbert, and much to everyone's surprise, a jury found him guilty. "We gave him charity on the first shot," one of the jurors explained. "He was upset and overcome psychologically. But it was the second bullet that did it. That was premeditated." Although one of the jurors told the judge that they would like to recommend leniency, under Florida's sentencing scheme conviction brought a mandatory life sentence, of which twenty-five years had to be served before the prisoner would be eligible for parole.

Almost immediately, Gilbert's friends and family began a campaign to have the sentence commuted. The conviction and what seemed to many a Draconian sentence caused outrage across Florida and in much of the nation, especially in the light of other recent "mercy killings." Two years earlier, in the same Broward County courthouse, a grand jury refused to indict 79-year-old Hans Florian, who had wheeled his 62-year-old wife Johanna out of her room at a nearby hospital and then shot her in the head. Mrs. Florian had also suffered from Alzheimer's, and screamed continuously except when heavily sedated. In San Antonio, Texas, in 1982, Woodrow Wilson Collums, 69, received a ten-year probationary sentence after shooting his 72-year-old brother, who lay helpless in a nursing institution.

Over the next few years, Gilbert's case would stay in the national limelight. In 1987 Robert Young played Gilbert in a made-for-TV movie, entitled "Mercy or Murder," based on the case. Lawyers attempted several strategies to have the sentence overturned, but none succeeded. Finally, in August 1990, Governor Bob Martinez, who previously had opposed clemency, changed his mind. One factor may have been that Kelly Hancock, the prosecutor at the original trial, had visited Gilbert in prison and reported that the then 81-year-old man was in failing health. Gilbert left prison, but the ethical issues raised by his case have not been resolved.

———

Mercy killings—and to many people there is little difference between so-called mercy killing and physician-assisted suicide—upset many people. Some people objected on strictly moral grounds—murder is murder and should be punished, no matter what the motives. Some saw the law as clear on the matter: A person who takes an active role in causing another person's death, regardless of the motive, has committed homicide. Others found the issue more complex, and disturbing. Had Emily Gilbert known that her mental condition would deteriorate so badly, would she have wanted to live in that condition? If anyone would know, what choice would they make? If Emily Gilbert could have been queried, would she have thanked her husband for doing what he did? Would we if we were in her position? One aspect that confounds the debate over right to die and assisted suicide is the issue of quality of life.

Do people have the right to end their lives if they can no longer live as they wish? We are not talking of mundane things such as whether one can still be as slim and athletic at 50 as at 20, or whether one drives a new Mercedes or an old Chevy. If hiking and being in the outdoors have been the great joy of a person's life, and then he can no longer walk, or can walk only with great difficulty, does this warrant ending life? If a woman has been married to a man for fifty years, and their lives have been so intertwined that she cannot bear the thought of living alone, is that reason to die?

These are not idle questions, because running throughout the legal debate is the political contest, part of the cultural war that has rocked America for the last two decades. On one side are fundamentalist religious groups, often called the religious right, who see all life as precious and death a matter to be decided by God, not man. On the other side stand an assortment of groups—liberals and moderates, feminists and other rights activists—who believe in personal autonomy and choice. The debate in some ways began in the 1960s with demands by the young for the right to choose alternative lifestyles. While we may now laugh at some of the pictures of young men and women in bell-bottom jeans, tie-dyed shirts, and long hair, their call for the right to be different, to be let alone, soon reverberated in other areas as well.

Perhaps the signature issue of the culture war is abortion, which, as we shall see, is closely related to the questions of right to die and assisted suicide. Initially abortion did not arouse a great deal of opposition aside from the Catholic Church, which had long condemned the practice. In the 1960s a number of states began liberalizing their laws and making it legal for women to procure abortion. Then in 1973 the Supreme Court short-circuited this process, and in the landmark case of *Roe v. Wade* declared that a woman had a constitutional right to choose whether or not to carry a fetus to term. *Roe* stands as the culmination of a series of cases that established a constitutional right to privacy and that, if one applied the question to the right to die, would seem to indicate the people had significant rights in that area as well.

Much to everyone's surprise, the decision triggered a groundswell of opposition among conservative Protestant groups, who denounced it as the final betrayal of all that America had held dear and that had been lost in the turmoil of the 1960s. Soon the religious right, organized into such groups as the Moral Majority, Focus on Family, and the Christian Coalition, began agitating not only against abortion, but against sex education in school, against rights for homosexuals, and for the return of mandatory prayer and Bible reading in public schools.

They also became the most vociferous opponents of the right to die and especially of physician-assisted suicide. When in 1976 the California legislature debated a death-with-dignity bill making explicit patients' right to refuse life-protracting treatment, both the California Catholic Council and the California Pro-Life Council denounced it as a wedge for involuntary euthanasia. They saw it as a short step from killing the unborn to killing all those whom society found undesirable. The Pro-Life Council denounced the bill and its sponsor, and at a committee meeting a spokesman held up a copy of William L. Shirer's *The Rise and Fall of the Third Reich.* A newspaper carried a cartoon entitled "Womb to Tomb," showing Death carrying a doctor's bag labeled "abortion on demand" and "right to die." The fact that the statute did not legalize assisted suicide or allow doctors to prescribe lethal medication mattered not. Giving people the right to refuse treatment and accept death gave them a choice that belonged only in the hands of God.

There is, of course, a great deal of illogic here. If one literally believes that a person will die only when God decides, then it matters little if one turns off a machine or stops taking medication. If the hour of death is divinely determined, then nothing a man or woman can do will alter that fact. Similarly, there is an illogic to viewing getting treatment as accepting God's will. If

God wants a person to be sick, then isn't medical treatment an interference? Conservatives objected to a culture in which choice took precedence over divine will, leading to a lapse in moral standards. If a woman can choose to have an abortion, or a man can choose to hasten his death by declining treatment, then a moral universe governed by eternal divine commandments no longer exists. Relativism replaces absolutism, and each person becomes a god unto himself or herself. The idea, as one woman put it in defending choice, is that "God gave man free will and he should be allowed to use it freely."

After the bill won passage in California, other states followed suit, and the more states extended choice, the more conservatives fought to restrict it. Where supporters spoke about the quality of life, opponents talked about its sanctity. In states with large Catholic or fundamentalist Protestant populations, the battles to secure living wills or death-with-dignity legislation proved difficult, but in the end choice triumphed. The American people, on these issues at least, seemed united. Poll after poll has shown strong support for the right of individuals to accept their fate, to elect death rather than suffer a long, drawn-out dying process simply because medical technology can delay the inevitable.

But there is a significant difference between accepting the inevitable and hastening it by committing suicide, and there is a difference between a doctor's accepting a patient's wishes to terminate life support and a doctor's providing a lethal dose of medication. The question of assisted suicide as a legal issue will be explored throughout this book, but one also needs a cultural context in which to understand how a movement seeking legalization of assisted suicide developed.

After the seeming demise of pro-euthanasia groups at the end of World War II because of the revelations of Nazi atrocities, advocates of the good death kept a low profile in the 1940s and 1950s. But the activism of the 1960s and the demand for rights made it possible to once again discuss the issue publicly. Derek Humphry wrote a book about having helped his first wife kill herself to end her suffering from cancer, and found himself besieged by invitations to speak to audiences in the United States and many other countries. In 1980 Humphry founded the Hemlock Society to promote a right to suicide. By the 1990s the Hemlock Society claimed eighty-six chapters and more than 57,000 members. The society's periodical, the *Hemlock Quarterly,* has over 30,000 subscribers, and its pages include readers' letters describing how relatives killed themselves as well as practical advice on ending one's life.

Humphry originally feared prosecution under state laws that criminalized assistance in suicide. But when no one arrested him, he grew bolder, and in 1991 he published *Final Exit: The Practicalities of Self-deliverance and Assisted Suicide for the Dying.* Humphrey tried to make clear that he did not believe every elderly person, or everyone with a debilitating disease, should take their lives. Rather, he extolled "that most important of civil liberties: the option to govern our own lives, which includes the right to choose to die."

The slim book proved a publishing sensation, and stayed on the *New York Times* best-seller list for eighteen weeks. Bookstores reported they could not keep up with the demand, and the Hemlock Society printed one edition after another. Within five years of publication *Final Exit* had sold more than 600,000 copies, and one can still find it on the shelves of almost any decent-sized bookstore in the country. Commentators agreed that the sales of the book indicated a profound shift in public attitudes toward suicide. Many of the people who have bought and continue to buy the book are neither sick nor elderly; as one middle-aged woman put it, "When I'm dying, I want to be in control."

The suicide rate among the elderly is on the increase; people over 65 make up 13 percent of the population but account for 20 percent of reported suicides. It is likely that the actual rate is even higher, since the elderly who are on strong medication often have access to what amounts to a lethal dosage should they wish to use it. In the absence of any explicit evidence that an old man or woman has committed suicide, physicians may well list disease or old age on the death certificate. Another

{ *Lethal Judgments* }

group with a rising suicide rate is young men with AIDS. Even though medical research has begun developing powerful drugs to slow or even kill off the virus, these come too late for many who are HIV-infected.

For those with AIDS, for those with cancer, for those with Lou Gehrig's disease and other debilitating illnesses, for those who are growing feeble because of age and declining health, physician-assisted suicide seems the next and logical progression in the fight for individual autonomy, for choice. Society has not yet accepted that step, and one cannot predict when or whether it will. If it is acceptable and legal for a doctor to turn off life-support apparatus at the request of a patient, should it be legal to give a person who is not on life support a prescription for a lethal quantity of barbiturates? Is there a difference—ethically, morally, and legally? If the argument is that patients ought to be able to determine their treatment, then the choice to end life is the same whatever means are employed. It is an argument that scandalizes religious conservatives and appalls many physicians. It is also the argument that professor Lawrence Tribe of the Harvard Law School made to the United States Supreme Court in his effort to get the justices to recognize a constitutionally protected right to physician-assisted suicide. How that case made its way to the Supreme Court, and the legal and moral issues surrounding the right to die in general and physician-assisted suicide in particular, is the story we now tell.

CHAPTER 3

Establishing a Right to Die

On April 15, 1975, Karen Ann Quinlan, an attractive and vivacious young woman, went to a birthday party with some friends. She did not eat very much, but along with alcohol she ingested some drugs. Then she started "to act kind of strange," and her friends, thinking she was drunk, drove her home and put her to bed. A while later they returned to check on her and discovered that she was not breathing. They tried mouth-to-mouth resuscitation and called a rescue squad. A policeman who arrived with the rescue team managed to revive Karen Ann's breathing, but she remained comatose as they rushed her to Newton Memorial Hospital in suburban New Jersey.

Doctors never determined why the young woman had stopped breathing for several minutes, but during that time she suffered anoxia, a deprivation of adequate oxygen to the brain. To assist her in breathing, Dr. Paul McGee, in charge of the intensive care unit that evening, placed Karen Ann on a respirator. Then he told the family that all they could do was wait to see if she would awaken from the coma. She never did.

Although she had suffered brain damage, Karen Ann Quinlan did not have a flat electroencephalogram (EEG), which would have indicated brain death. In addition, she exhibited periodic involuntary muscle activity, and reflexively responded to various stimuli, such as light, sound, smell, and pain. But for three months she showed no sign of awakening, and her parents, Julia and Joseph Quinlan, spent much of that time at her bedside praying for her recovery. Finally they decided that Karen Ann had suffered enough, and signed a release to allow the doctors to take her off the respirator. "I'm convinced," Joe Quinlan said, "it is our Lord's will that Karen be allowed to die."

The doctors, even though they believed the young woman would never recover, refused to removed the breathing apparatus, fearing that they might be held liable for murder. Joseph Quinlan then went to court to secure authority to discontinue all extraordinary medical measures. What had been a private nightmare for the Quinlan family became the opening round in an ongoing national debate.

At the trial the family called a number of expert witnesses who told how doctors routinely allowed terminally ill patients to die. Dr. Julius Korein, a neurologist, described "judicious neglect," in which a doctor would in essence say, "Don't treat this patient anymore [since] it does not serve either the patient, the family or society in any meaningful way to continue treatment." Dr. Korein also explained to the court, and through them to the millions of readers who followed the trial in the nation's newspapers, about DNR, the instructions a doctor would put on a terminally ill patient's chart, meaning "Do Not Resuscitate."

Despite what appeared to be an overwhelming body of evidence in support of the Quinlans' petition, the trial court refused to approve taking Karen off the respirator. Judge Robert Muir ruled, "There is a duty to continue life-assisting apparatus. There is no constitutional right to die that can be asserted by a parent for his incompetent adult child."

On appeal, however, the New Jersey Supreme Court reversed, holding that one could find a "right to die" not only in the common law, but in the more recently enunciated right to privacy, which the Supreme Court had announced in the 1965 case of *Griswold v. Connecticut.* The transcript of oral argument clearly indicates not only that the judges were seeking the right legal decision, but that they well understood the human issues of suffering involved. At one point Justice Morris Pashman exclaimed, "Really doesn't the horror of continued pseudo-life cry out for some type of handling, some type of treatment by a court?"

A key issue that the judges kept coming back to is why couldn't the hospital and the doctors simply follow the wishes of the parents? There would be no liability, one judge suggested, if after consulting with the Quinlans they discontinued life support. Why should they object to that? "Simply because there is a duty on their part," the hospital's lawyer responded. Doctors have a duty to save life, not to end it. This theme, which made little impression on the New Jersey court, would become a refrain in the debate over physician-assisted suicide two decades later.

By the end of oral argument, it seemed clear that the state's highest court wanted to rule in favor of the Quinlans, although it remained unclear on what grounds they would base that decision. As one member of the court noted, "This case should never have been started, but it was started, and it's here. Usually we try to contribute something towards a solution. I guess that's our primary and ultimate function here."

On March 31, 1976, the Supreme Court of the State of New Jersey handed down its historic ruling that people have a constitutionally protected right to die and that this right can be exercised for them in situations where the patient can no longer make such decisions. In its unanimous opinion, the Court declared, "We have no doubt that if Karen were herself miraculously lucid for an interval . . . and perceptive of her irreversible condition, she would effectively decide upon discontinuance of the life-support apparatus, even if it meant the prospect of natural death."

Where Judge Muir had refused to take into account the subjective aspects of the case—the suffering of Karen Ann and of her family—the high court had made that very subjectivity central to its decision. The quality of life, even for a person in a permanent coma, who by all accounts felt no pain, could be used as the starting point for determining the legal issues.

But what about the state's long-acknowledged right to preserve life? Did the court simply dismiss it as irrelevant and outdated? Anticipating the reasoning the U.S. Supreme Court would later invoke in the series of abortion cases, the New Jersey court laid down a balancing test in which to weigh the state's interests and those of the individual. "We think the State's interest [to preserve life] weakens and the individual's right to privacy grows as the degree of bodily invasion increases and the prognosis dims. Ultimately, there comes a point at which the individual's rights overcome the state interest." As Peter Filene has noted, "This was truly historic. In keeping with the egalitarian revolution that courts and legislatures had been waging on behalf of blacks, women, and the poor, the New Jersey Supreme Court was proclaiming the principle of equal rights in the arena of health. Medical paternalism was converted into a democratic process whereby family members could speak for incompetent patients."

In re Quinlan focused national attention on questions that have continued to concern Americans to this day. What rights does an individual have in refusing treatment, even if that refusal leads to death? Who can make medical decisions for a person who is legally incompetent? Can a person legally secure assistance in dying? These are all, of course, questions of law, but there is no area of the law more fraught with ethical and moral considerations than the right to die. While the establishment of a legal right to die often seems focused around the cases of two young women, Karen Ann Quinlan and Nancy Beth Cruzan, in fact its roots run deep in Anglo-American common law. It is buttressed by the more recent elaboration of liberty interests embedded in the Fourteenth Amendment's Due Process Clause.

The Quinlan case led the general public to assume that the law had not kept pace with the rapid technological advances then transforming medical practice. After nearly two decades of civil rights activism, by the mid-seventies many people believed that there must be some constitutional right to die, that among the rights explicitly and implicitly protected by the Constitution there had to be protection of individual autonomy. The Supreme Court had ruled that men and women enjoy a constitutionally protected right to privacy; that women have a constitutional right to obtain an abortion; and that even persons accused of heinous crimes have a constitutional right to decent treatment at the hands of the police and a fair trial in the courts. Certainly, then, people thought, Americans *must* have a constitutional right to die in peace and with dignity if they so chose.[1]

Eventually, the United States Supreme Court would agree that a limited right existed, but not until 1990. Nonetheless, one can find legal support for a right to die well before *Quinlan.* Since then there has been legislation regulating and protecting health care decisions in Congress and in nearly every state. At the beginning of the twenty-first century it is this law that governs end of life choices for most Americans.

Prior to *Quinlan,* most law affecting personal health care decisions grew out of the common law. Over the centuries judges have often had to face new situations without the guidance of legislation. They have decided these cases on a mixture of statutory law they considered relevant, the precedents of other cases relating to the subject, and common sense. While in a democracy legislatures obviously have the responsibility to determine public policy, often legislation lags behind social reality, and the courts are called upon to render judgments. If the legislature agrees with the judicial determination, it may not even bother to enact legislation, and the judge-made, or common, law remains in force.

Common law has long held that an individual enjoys a right to be free from physical harm, and over the course of years this

---

[1]Although the phrase "right to die" has become a commonplace, and is used throughout this book, the reader should be aware that it is not as clear as one might think. For lawyers and judges, the term "right" has a high, almost sacred, status. Health care professionals, on the other hand, often equate "right" with "duty," a situation that when applied to death may be confusing. The President's Commission for the Study of Ethical Problems in Medicine and Biomedical and Behavioral Research chose to use "foregoing life-sustaining treatment," a phrase that while technically more accurate is unwieldy and has definitional problems of its own. Moreover, since the debate has expanded to include assisted suicide, the issue is not just whether a person may forgo treatment, but whether a person may actively seek treatment that will lead to death.

right expanded to include the notion that unauthorized medical treatment constituted assault and battery. "Under a free government," an Illinois court declared in 1905, "the free citizen's first and greatest right, which underlies all others—the right to the inviolability of his person—is the subject of universal acquiescence, and this right necessarily forbids a physician or surgeon ... to violate without permission, the bodily integrity of his patient by ... operating upon him without his consent or knowledge."

In a Minnesota case that same year that is still studied by first-year law students, a court ruled that a doctor could not, in the absence of an emergency, perform an unauthorized procedure. "If the operation was performed without plaintiff's consent, and the circumstances were not such as to justify its performance without, it was wrongful; and if it was wrongful, it was unlawful." Benjamin Cardoza of New York, who served on the U.S. Supreme Court in the 1930s and is considered by many the finest common law jurist of this century, declared that "Every human being of adult years and sound mind has a right to determine what shall be done with his own body."

Common law spoke less to the idea of a "right to die" than to the question of individual autonomy, the control that a person has over his or her body against unwanted action, be it brute physical attack or medical intrusion. A person has a right to consent to treatment, and thus has a corollary right to refuse care. However, in this as in so many areas of the law, what appears simple on the surface is hedged about by conditions. The law recognizes that there may be times when a right, no matter how important, may be circumscribed or when a person may be unable to exercise a right.

At the heart of the law is the idea of informed consent. If a person is to make intelligent decisions about whether to accept or decline particular therapies, there must be adequate information upon which to base that judgment, and this requires that the physician talk to and consult with the patient. While today this sounds reasonable, not that many years ago doctors did not feel it necessary to discuss medical decisions with their patients, nor even in many instances to seek their permission. Even to-day, many doctors view the idea of informed consent as no more than a duty to warn about any possible undesirable effects of treatment in order to avoid malpractice suits. One still finds doctors who claim that patients are incapable of understanding medical issues and that trying to explain complicated procedures in lay terms is a waste of time.

While doctors and hospitals routinely require consent forms for almost any type of procedure, these forms are worthless unless it can be shown that certain conditions have been met. A signature on a piece of paper does not by itself prove informed consent. For consent to be informed, it must be *voluntarily* given by a *competent* person who *understands* what is involved. These ideas are not unique to health care, but have evolved in many areas of law, including contracts as well as torts.

Valid consent may be given only by someone who has the mental capacity to make that decision. By this the law does not mean a specific level of intelligence or require that a person make the "right" decision, since what is "right" will depend upon each individual's beliefs and attitudes. For one person, consenting to chemotherapy may be the correct choice; for an-other, declining the treatment may be the better option. Most courts have moved toward the definition of "capacity" given in the *Restatement of Torts:* the ability to appreciate the nature, extent, or probable consequences of the physician's conduct for which consent is sought.[2]

A person must understand that to which he or she is consent-ing, and here the complex nature of medical treatment, as well as the uncertainty of results, makes understanding a most diffi-cult criterion. How much does a doctor have to tell a patient in order for the patient to understand what is at risk and what a

---

[2]The *Restatements* are the periodic attempts by the American Law Institute to define what the current legal consensus is in major areas of the law. While they have no legal standing per se, judges often rely on *Re-statements* when seeking workable definitions of particular issues.

{ *Lethal Judgments* }

procedure will entail? How technical must the physician be, or must the information be given in a form that any layperson can grasp? Is it possible to predict with accuracy what the risks are from certain drugs or procedures?

By now nearly all states have imposed upon physicians a duty to inform a patient of the risks and benefits associated with treatment, as well as what that treatment implies, and there is a clear legal duty to do so in a comprehensible manner. Not only must a patient consent to the care, but it must be informed consent. There is no legal defense to battery based on consent if a patient's consent to touching [treatment] is given "without sufficient knowledge and understanding of the nature of the touching." Physicians who fail to carry out the duty to inform leave themselves open to malpractice suits.

But jurisdictions differ over what test they will use to determine if sufficient information has been given. About half the states use what is known as a customary professional practice test, in which expert witnesses would testify as to whether the amount of information a doctor had given, and the manner in which it had been given, was according to customary practice. Recently there has been a shift toward a legal, or "reasonable person," standard: namely, whether the doctor provided sufficient information and in such a way that a reasonable layperson would understand the risks involved. This would be determined not by expert witnesses, but by the fact finder—the judge or jury.

Ideally, doctors and their patients ought to engage in a collaborative decision-making process in which the doctor would spell out his or her judgment on proper treatment and explain what it involved, and the competent patient would voluntarily make an informed decision as to whether to go forward with the recommendation. But the world is far from ideal, and the law has spelled out four exceptions to the informed consent rule.

The first is emergency care. In a critical situation requiring immediate action, a doctor may treat an injured or ill person without the consent of that person or of those authorized to make that consent, such as parents of a minor. Here the law recognizes that delay may cause the loss of life, and common sense tells us that if there is time to describe treatment and discuss risks and benefits, there probably is no emergency. But because emergencies do not allow for discussion, and in many cases even for securing information, decisions may be made here that the patient, had he or she been competent, might have opposed.

If a patient is incompetent, then informed consent is by definition impossible to obtain, and this negates the doctor's duty to inform as well. However, it is not always easy to determine when someone is incompetent. Patients who are unconscious obviously are unable to involve themselves in any meaningful decision making, as are those who are inebriated, delirious, or in some form of toxic stupor. The hard cases are those where a patient is conscious but somehow impaired, so that it will be difficult to tell if he or she understands what is happening.

Another exception is the therapeutic privilege, which permits a physician to withhold information if such disclosure would not be in the patient's best interest or would prevent the doctor from providing appropriate care. While at first glance this seems an open invitation for a doctor to deny information on the subjective judgment that it would be harmful for the patient to know, this is not the way the privilege has been interpreted by the courts. This exception, which has not been the subject of much litigation, is addressed primarily to those instances where the emotional shock of the news might trigger the very crisis the doctor is trying to avoid.

Finally, as with all rights, a person may waive the right; however, as with informed consent, waiver must be voluntary and informed, and the person must be competent. Given the current emphasis on self-determination and collaboration with the doctor in treatment, it would seem strange that people might not want the information they need to make such decisions. But as Alan Meisel points out, it may be a manifestation of autonomy. Giving patients the information they need to make decisions is one form of self-determination. "However, compelling them to receive information they do not want or to make decisions they do not wish to make is a paternalistic denial of the right of self-determination. Waiver is the patient's counterpart to the therapeutic privilege." Just as patients have the right to consent or withhold consent, so they have a right to participate in decision making or to put their trust and their lives in the hands of another.

———

During the 1970s, as the public debate over the right to die expanded, doctors found themselves in something of a legal dilemma. On the one hand, they could be sued for malpractice if they forced treatment on an unwilling patient or failed in their duty to inform a patient of the risks and benefits associated with a particular therapy. On these issues the law seemed clear enough. At the same time, doctors worried that they might be liable to criminal action if they halted a treatment already begun, such as by removing a respirator or a feeding tube. It is one thing to withhold life-sustaining treatment, especially if a competent patient makes it clear that he or she does not want it. Legally, that would be the equivalent of passive euthanasia, allowing nature to take its course and death to bring its peace. Turning off a respirator, however, might be viewed as active euthanasia, which morally and legally could be considered murder.

That this concern worried doctors could be seen in the oral argument before the New Jersey Supreme Court in the Quinlan case. Judge Sidney Schreiber asked the Quinlans' attorney, Paul Armstrong, whether he wasn't requesting the court to declare that if the doctors terminated treatment, they would be subject to neither civil nor criminal consequences. When Armstrong agreed, Chief Justice Richard J. Hughes leaned forward and asked:

"Mr. Armstrong, doesn't it come down to this, the long and short of it being that you ask the Court to declare the law to be—there having been no precedent in any part of the common law that I can figure—that the Court is to declare now that if the doctors stop this procedure and cause death that it will not result in any civil or criminal sanctions as to such doctors, or indeed as to such family members."

ARMSTRONG: "Yes, Your Honor."

HUGHES: "So that, in effect, you're asking the Court to make new law."

ARMSTRONG: "On these facts, that's correct."

HUGHES: ". . . In that case, Mr. Armstrong, wouldn't the Court be legislating?"

ARMSTRONG: "No, Your Honor. It would be reflecting the majesty of the evolution of the common law, as it has since its inception in England. I genuinely think that the Court is fully competent to address itself to these types of problems."

It appears that a number of right to die cases, where the doctors and family both believed it would be best to terminate life support, went to court not to resolve questions of personal autonomy but to ensure that neither the medical professionals nor the hospitals faced civil or criminal liability. There has been only one instance in which there was a prosecution for stopping life-support treatment at the patient's or family's request, and that indictment was eventually dismissed.

In May 1981 Clarence Herbert, a 55-year-old security guard, underwent surgery in a Los Angeles hospital to correct an intestinal obstruction. In the recovery room he suffered cardiopulmonary arrest and lapsed into a coma from which he never regained consciousness. Three days later his physicians, Robert Nedjl and Neil Barber, adjudged his condition "hopeless" and informed his family. Herbert's wife and eight children all agreed that he should be taken off the machines, since he had indicated to them that he did not wish to be kept alive by a respirator. The doctors disconnected Herbert but, like Karen Quinlan, he remained comatose yet able to breathe by himself. After further consultation, the family and the doctors agreed that intravenous feeding should be stopped, and Herbert died six days later.

Subsequently the Los Angeles county prosecutor charged Nedjl and Barber with murder, claiming that they had cut off the respirator and feeding in order to cover up their malpractice and save money for a prepaid health plan. The doctors claimed that they did no more than follow the wishes of the family in an irreversible coma case. The magistrate who initially heard the case dismissed the charges, but a superior court reinstated them, only to be reversed by the court of appeals.

The appellate court, while recognizing the emotional distinction often made between a respirator and a feeding tube, considered both to be forms of medical treatment. In this case, the court ruled, the doctors—in consultation with the family—had withdrawn "heroic" life supports, and the court viewed this as an act not of comission but of omission, allowing nature to take its course. The court asked what is, or should be, a central question in all such cases: What is the duty that a physician owes to the patient? Obviously a doctor should do nothing positive, such as injecting a patient with a poison, for that would be a deliberate act of murder. But a doctor does not owe a patient the duty of heroic treatment, nor is there an obligation to impose or continue treatment against the wishes of the patient or of the family.

In fact, despite wording in criminal codes that would, on the face of it, make physicians liable for acts of omission as well as comission, no court has ever ruled that withholding or withdrawing life support constitutes a criminal act. A doctor will be protected, the Massachusetts Supreme Judicial Court noted, "if he acts on a good faith judgment that is not grievously unreasonable by medical standards."

Why should this be so? If a doctor turns off a resuscitator, and the patient dies as a result, is this any different than if the doctor had taken a gun and shot the patient? The prevailing legal view is that the real cause of death is not the termination of life-sustaining treatment, but the underlying illness. The disease, and not the doctor, killed the victim, so there can be no homicide. This is the reasoning ultimately adopted by the New Jersey court in *Quinlan*. Yet both medical and legal ethicists have problems with this rationale, since it could, if taken literally, allow any patient to refuse any treatment and allow any physician to withhold treatment, even a procedure that might save the patient's life. Such a policy would go against the state's long recognized power to protect the interests and well-being of its citizens and to intervene on their behalf when necessary.

Some courts have reasoned that there can be no homicide if a patient exercises his or her right to forgo treatment. This is the underlying philosophy in the Uniform Rights of the Terminally Ill Act, sec. 10(a), that "death resulting from the withholding or withdrawal of life-sustaining treatment pursuant to a declaration and in accordance with this [act] does not constitute, for any purpose, a suicide or a homicide."[3] This or a similar provision can be found in the natural death acts adopted by most states. Such acts provide a statutory framework in which patients can determine their treatment and which shields physicians from liability for respecting these decisions.

These laws also hold surrogates free of liability, an issue that arose in the *Quinlan* case and that is involved in any situation of a patient who, like Karen Quinlan, cannot make an informed decision because of legal incompetency. The law has for decades dealt with "persons under a disability," be it because of age or mental or physical infirmity, through the appointment of guardians. It has also recognized the right of people to name their own surrogates to act under certain conditions, the most common situation the appointment of executors to carry out the terms of a will.

Family members of a legally disabled person are normally accepted by the courts as surrogates. As the Florida Supreme Court noted, "if there are close family members such as the patient's spouse, adult children, or parents, who are willing to exercise this right on behalf of the patient, there is no requirement that a guardian be judicially appointed." There are, however, some judges who believe that only a court-appointed guardian, acting together with the doctor, should be allowed to make life-and-death decisions, even if the guardian is a close member of the family. Most jurisdictions, however, are willing

---

[3]Uniform acts are proposals made by the State Commissioners for Uniform Legislation, a body that has now been meeting for over a century, which drafts model acts on issues of common concern. While the states are free to adopt, reject, or amend the proposed legislation, many states do in fact adopt them, thus providing uniformity from one state to another on a number of important matters.

to leave the process to family, with judicial intervention only if particular circumstances require it.

It is through surrogates that the law has extended to incompetent patients a right to refuse life-sustaining treatment, and it did this starting with *Quinlan*. The New Jersey court declared that "our affirmation of Karen's independent right of choice . . . would ordinarily be based upon her competency to assert it. The sad truth, however, is that she is grossly incompetent and we cannot discern her supposed choice. . . . Nevertheless we have concluded that Karen's right of privacy may be asserted on her behalf by her guardian under the peculiar circumstances here present."

As a result, right to die cases have from the start assumed that incompetent patients have the same right as competent patients, but that informed consent must be secured in a different manner, either through previous declaration or through the decision of a surrogate or guardian.

By the time the New Jersey Supreme Court heard the Quinlan case in 1976, in addition to well-established common law rules on informed consent and guardianship, it could also look to a new constitutional basis, the right to privacy first enunciated by the U.S. Supreme Court in the landmark decision of *Griswold v. Connecticut* (1965) and expanded in the high court's abortion ruling in *Roe v. Wade* (1973). New Jersey Chief Justice Richard J. Hughes drew upon these two cases to conclude that the federal Constitution guarantees certain areas of privacy, and "presumably this right is broad enough to encompass a patient's decision to decline medical treatment under certain circumstances."

Cases following *Quinlan* drew upon both the common law right of personal autonomy and the constitutional right of privacy. In recent years, however, criticism by conservatives of a federal constitutional right of privacy has led many courts to back away from reliance on *Griswold* and rely on the older common law rights. While some state courts, relying on state-guaranteed rights of privacy, continue to uphold such a right, federal courts, and especially the Supreme Court, talk more about autonomy than privacy.

We can thus see that although right to die cases are relatively new, a sufficient body of legal precedents existed for judges to confront these cases with the assurance that the law they expounded relied on established principles. In many instances the courts admitted that they were making new law, and invited the legislature to enact legislation clarifying the issues and enunciating the state's interests in these decisions. Most states did respond with so-called living will or natural death statutes, but these did not by themselves create new rights; rather, they codified already existing common law rights and spelled out more precise procedures for dealing with legally incompetent patients. What we find, then, is a series of decisions that intertwine common law principles, statutory regulations, and constitutional principles.

The year after *Quinlan* the Massachusetts Supreme Judicial Court heard the case of Joseph Saikewicz, a 67-year-old man with an IQ of 10, who was suffering from acute myeloblastic leukemia. Doctors said that without treatment Saikewicz would live for a few months at most, and probably without great pain or suffering. With chemotherapy, he had a 30 to 50 percent chance of remission for up to fifteen months, but the treatment itself would be painful and produce uncomfortable side effects. The patient himself would not understand the reason for the treatment and, because of the pain, probably would not cooperate.

The court-appointed guardian had recommended against the treatment, and the probate court agreed that it would not be in the patient's best interest. The probate judge noted, among other things, the patient's right to privacy, his age and condition, and the poor quality of life available to him even if the treatment proved successful. The state's high court affirmed the ruling but rejected the idea that quality of life should be a consideration; neither intelligence nor social standing had any bearing on the value of life insofar as the law was concerned. Judge Paul J. Liacos based his decision on a cost/benefit analysis, the pain and suffering of the treatment against the limited benefits that would accrue, and concluded it would be in Saikewicz's best interests not to be treated. As in *Quinlan*, the court emphasized the importance of personal autonomy and the right of the patient to determine his own fate or, as in this case, to rely on substituted judgment.

Where Saikewicz's case differed from Quinlan's, however, is in the Massachusetts court's insistence that the ultimate authority in deciding for incompetents rested with the judiciary. While the wishes of the family or of a guardian or the recommendation of a hospital ethics committee would be given serious consideration, the final decision would be in the hands of a court, and would thus require some form of adversarial hearing in which the interests of the patient would be represented. Doctors, of course, objected to this decision, since it would make them defend their medical decisions in a highly sensitive area and bring in one more party to the decision-making process.

Recognizing at least some validity in their complaint, a Massachusetts appellate court later held that hospitals and doctors did not need court permission for "No Code" and "Do Not Resuscitate" ("DNR") orders. The case involved an elderly woman, Shirly Dinnerstein, who suffered from Alzheimer's and the results of a massive stroke that had left her in a vegetative state. Both her adult children argued that if a cardiac or respiratory arrest occurred, she should not be resuscitated. Following *Saikewicz,* the family, the attending physician, and the hospital joined in a suit to determine if "DNR" orders required court approval, and the court ruled that such decisions remained in the realm of medical judgment and the family's wishes.

Next to Karen Ann Quinlan, probably no other case attracted as much public attention as did that of Brother Charles Fox of the Catholic Order of the Society of Mary. Brother Fox, 83, suffered a hernia while tending his garden in August 1979; during surgery at Nassau Hospital he went into cardiopulmonary arrest that led to anoxia, the loss of oxygen to the brain, and the doctors placed him on a respirator. A few years earlier, while discussing the Quinlan case, Brother Fox had told his close friend and spiritual adviser, Father Philip Eichner, that should he become terminally ill and incompetent, he did not wish to be kept alive by extraordinary means. Father Eichner, attempting to carry out his friend's wishes, asked that the respirator be removed.

Two neurosurgeons agreed that Brother Fox would never recover, but the hospital refused to disconnect the respirator. So Father Eichner went to court, seeking appointment as Brother Fox's guardian. The trial court agreed to the request, and while denying the relevance of any constitutional right of privacy, it found that common law rights of bodily self-determination would allow termination of treatment. Father Eichner, as guardian, could now exercise that right for his friend.

The local district attorney, Dennis Dillon, decided to appeal the decision, but before the court of appeals, New York's highest court, could rule on the appeal, Brother Fox died of congestive heart failure on January 24, 1980. Although the high court could have ruled the case moot, that is, no longer a controversy, it decided to take the appeal on the grounds that such a question was likely to recur. In its ruling, the court of appeals wrote what was at that time the strongest judicial support ever made for a right to die.

Speaking for a near-unanimous court, Judge Sol Wachtler held that life support could be withdrawn from an incompetent who had, when competent, clearly and convincingly declared that he or she would not want to be kept alive by heroic measures in a terminal illness. Further, for such wishes to be carried out, neither judicial hearings nor any other special procedures were necessary, provided there was clear and convincing evidence of the patient's wishes. However, Wachtler and his colleagues were not willing to infer such intent in the absence of such evidence, nor were they willing to allow others, even family members, to make that decision, no matter how persuasively the circumstances argued that termination of life support would be in the best interests of the patient and of society.

The court did not use quite these words, but it made its position quite clear in this and in an accompanying case it ruled on at the same time. Fifty-two-year-old John Storar was mentally retarded and suffered from advanced cancer of the bladder and a related loss of blood. His mother asked that the transfusions be stopped. In denying her request, the court said, "Although we understand and respect his mother's despair ... a court should not in the circumstances of this case allow an incompetent patient to bleed to death because someone, even someone as close as a parent or sibling, feels that this is best for one with an incurable disease."

While the Brother Fox case strongly reinforced the common law right of self-determination, it required the person's wishes to have been made known clearly and convincingly. But the ruling also seemed to close the door on any hope for incompetents, especially the mentally retarded, who had never been in a position to make their desires known, even shutting out parents or guardians from acting for them. Throughout the decade, courts and legislatures would differ over who should make these life-or-death choices and what evidence, if any, would be needed to support those decisions.

Karen Quinlan, Joseph Saikewicz, and Brother Fox could not, at the time of their ordeals, participate in the decision making. But Abe Perlmutter could, and when the Florida Medical Center refused to honor his choice, he went to court.

Perlmutter, a retired cabdriver, suffered from amyotrophic lateral sclerosis, commonly called Lou Gehrig's disease, a progressive deterioration and hardening of the portions of the spinal cord, leading to loss of muscle control and ultimately paralysis. Perlmutter relied on a respirator to sustain his breathing, and while his body may have been ravaged, his mind remained clear; he easily met the law's definition of competency. He knew that if taken off the respirator he would live only a few hours; with it he might live as long as two years. After consultation with his family and doctor, Perlmutter asked to be disconnected, but the hospital refused.

The circuit judge who heard the case, John G. Ferris, declared Perlmutter competent, defended his constitutional right to privacy, and ordered the hospital not to interfere with the patient's decision to disconnect. The hospital appealed, but the appellate court affirmed. While recognizing the hospital's legitimate fear of incurring liability, it ruled that Perlmutter's rights of privacy and self-determination outweighed those considerations. On October 6, 1978, the respirator was disconnected. An alarm sounded, and Perlmutter's son turned it off. With his family at his side, Abe Perlmutter died.

One issue, how do we know what people want, has been satisfactorily answered, or to be more precise, could be. Americans now have available to them so-called living wills, by which they can make advance determinations of what kind of health care they want should they become incapacitated. Living wills, or advance directives, are relatively recent phenomena. An Illinois attorney, Luis Kutner, is given credit for proposing a formal advance directive in 1969, although the idea did not immediately catch on. Following the Quinlan case, however, interest grew rapidly, and that growth in turn created new legal problems that took the better part of a decade to sort through.

Although the phrase "living will" is in common use, such documents normally incorporate one or more types of advance directives. The law starts with the assumption that each individual is the person best able to make decisions about his or her health care. In normal circumstances, a competent individual, who has been informed about specific treatments and risks, chooses whether to go forward or not. This type of informed consent, however, takes place simultaneously with the need to accept or forgo treatment. A person becomes ill or injured, a doctor prescribes a certain procedure or therapy, and the decision is made. While the time frame may extend over a few days or weeks depending upon the severity of the problem, for practical purposes all of the events happen contemporaneously.

Advance directives, on the other hand, are anticipatory. A person says in effect, "If something happens to me and I am, for whatever reason, unable to decide for myself, then given certain circumstances, this is what I would decide." The directions are contingent upon certain types of events occuring; because one cannot know the future, it is impossible to be entirely precise.

{ *Lethal Judgments* }

In addition, through a durable power of attorney, the person may say that if he or she is unable to act, then a surrogate is empowered to make those decisions.

The legal basis for advance directives derives from the same common law and constitutional basis as that supporting the right to die—the right of individual autonomy. Competent people should be able to make their own decisions, with substituted judgment permitted for incompetent patients. When a person indicates his or her wishes, if the person becomes incompetent, then the surrogate may act to carry out those wishes.

The idea of living wills spread quickly, because it relieved health care providers and the courts from having to endure litigation on a case-by-case basis. By 1992, all fifty states and the District of Columbia had adopted some form of living-will statute. The problem is that even though one can now decide for oneself what sort of care one would want should there be a terrible accident or the onset of a debilitating disease, only a small minority of Americans have written advance directives. When a tragedy strikes, in the absence of an advance directive the burden is on family members to guess what their loved one would have wanted.

During the decade of the eighties the public might well have become confused had it attempted to make some sense out of the welter of litigation confronting the courts. But in fact some trends could be discerned.

First, a competent patient had the right to terminate treatment, although courts differed on whether this right derived from common law rules of self-determination, the constitutional protection of privacy, or both.

Second, if a formerly competent person had made a clear and convincing statement of intent, those wishes would be honored, and in most jurisdictions there would be no need to involve the courts in the decision-making process. The adoption by most states of living-will or death-with-dignity statutes had made it possible for a person to make choices against the contingency of future disaster with a reasonable certainty that such wishes would be honored.

Third, the hard cases, and the ones that caught the headlines, involved incompetent patients who either had never been competent or when competent had left no indication of their wishes. Here courts had to grapple with the most difficult of legal and moral questions, trying to balance the state's interest in preserving life with what would be best for the individual, while also taking into account the judgments and fears of the health care providers.

At the core of the debate is the question of who decides if the individual is unable to do so—the family, the doctor, the hospital and its ethics committee, a judge, or some other party? What criteria should they use? What if their own beliefs run counter to those of the patient? How great a role should courts, as opposed to state legislatures, play in the process? When, if ever, is it more beneficial for the patient or for society to "pull the plug?" What happens if the best interests of the patient do not coincide with what appear to be the best interests of society? Is society best served by preserving life in all instances? Is there a slippery slope, so that allowing a person in severe pain to die today may lead to allowing less-afflicted people to die tomorrow, and the merely elderly or infirm the day after?

While a few courts have indicated that extensive judicial involvement is necessary, for the most part judges have not been eager to intrude into what they see as a legitimate function of family and doctors. At the same time, courts, as protectors of individual rights and construers of legislation, must be concerned that such decisions meet legal and statutory requirements, that adequate information is available, that due concern has been paid to the dignity of the patient.

For most people, a key concern is the "quality of life," yet here indeed one finds a slippery slope. Different people have greatly varying views on what is an acceptable quality of life. Thus in the case of Earle Spring, a 78-year-old senile patient dependent on dialysis treatments, the family petitioned the courts to end the treatment, claiming that were he lucid, such would be his choice. In opposition, a court-appointed guardian argued that no evidence existed to support this contention. Ultimately the Massachusetts high court sided with the guardian since it had no evidence of what Spring might have wanted when competent, although in doing so it did not dismiss the value of substituted judgment by family. The opinion, however, more than most in this area, spoke of the patient's irreversible mental deterioration, which, aside from kidney failure, would never be restored to a "normal, cognitive, integrated, functioning existence." This led George Annas to charge that the court's view, "phrased another way, [is that] there are some categories of people who are so abnormal or ill-functioning that the state has no interest in seeing to it that their lives are preserved."

———

Almost all of these cases, and many others involving termination of treatment, were appealed to the United States Supreme Court, on grounds that a federal right—privacy—was implicated. But the high court consistently refused to grant certiorari, and since the Court rarely indicates why it turns down a petition, one can only surmise the reasons. Nearly all cases arose in state courts, and in most of them the court reached its decision on either common law principles or state constitutional or statutory grounds; unless there is a clear violation of federal law, federal courts will not normally review state court decisions based on "adequate state grounds."

However, many state court decisions referred to a right to privacy that, after *Griswold,* seemed to be grounded in the federal constitution. But in the 1980s, the Supreme Court grew increasingly distrustful of a constitutionally protected right of privacy, and the conservative justices appointed by Ronald Reagan expressed reservations over *Griswold* and especially over *Roe v. Wade,* the abortion decision. They questioned whether, in the absence of a specific provision, a right to privacy actually existed in the Constitution.

Ironically, even as the public accepted the idea of a constitutionally protected right of privacy, the Court sought other legal grounds to support self-determination. Court opinions spoke less and less about privacy, focusing instead on the notion of autonomy. With the increasing litigation and publicity surrounding right to die questions, it was only a matter of time before the Court agreed to hear a case. The justices took that opportunity in the case of Nancy Cruzan.

On January 11, 1983, coming home from her job on the night shift at a cheese factory, 25-year-old Nancy Beth Cruzan lost control of her old Nash Rambler on an icy road near the small town of Carthage, Missouri. The car slid off the road and flipped over, throwing her some thirty-five feet out of the car and face down into a ditch. Emergency help came promptly, but not soon enough. As her father, Joe Cruzan, said, "If only the ambulance had arrived five minutes earlier—or five minutes later." The rescue squad resuscitated Nancy Cruzan, but by then her brain had been deprived of oxygen for too long.

Nancy, who in so many ways resembled the once vivacious Karen Quinlan, now suffered a similar fate. She never regained consciousness, and sank into a persistent vegetative state, seemingly awake, but totally unaware of her surroundings. From time to time there would be reflexive movement, but despite the hours that her parents Joyce and Joe Cruzan spent at her bedside hoping for some sign of cognition, they could not see any. For seven years Nancy Cruzan lay curled in a fetal position at the Missouri Rehabilitation Center in Mount Vernon, kept alive by a tube into her stomach providing nutrients and water. She had been a healthy person before the accident, and her doctors said that her heart and lungs could function for thirty years.

The Cruzans, however, did not consider this half-existence to be life, and they went to court asking that the feeding tube be removed to allow Nancy to die. The case differed from earlier ones primarily in the fact that no artificial machines kept Nancy alive; her heart beat, and she could breathe on her own. She, like some 10,000 other people in persistent vegetative states, needed only food, and in essence, removing the feeding tube would mean that she would starve to death. Although the American Medical Association and many medical ethicists consider artificial feeding and hydration a medical treatment that, like a respirator, can be withdrawn from a terminally ill patient, the idea horrified many people. Food and water, even through a tube, are the basic necessities of life, and evoke a far more emotional response than do respirators.

The Cruzan case *(Cruzan v. Director, Missouri Department of Health)* brought together many of the strands of earlier decisions: questions of personal autonomy, surrogate decision making, the state's interests in preserving life, and the growing conflict between medical technology and humane values. Daniel Callahan, the director of the Hastings Institute, which has been the center for much research into ethical issues associated with the right to die, noted that in *Cruzan* and similar cases, one sees the clash of two basic values. "One is the sanctity of life, with its religious roots; the other is the technological imperative to do everything possible to save a life."

But while Nancy was technically "alive," did she have a life? Her parents did not believe so; they considered their daughter to be trapped in a cage and themselves to have the obligation—and the right—to free her from that prison. If Nancy were alive, Joe Cruzan said, she would say, "Help, get me out of this." George Annas, of the Boston University Medical School, agreed: "The technological imperative obliterates the person altogether. It acts as if the person doesn't exist—that she has no personality, no family, and that no one who loves her can make decisions about her."

When it became clear that Nancy would never recover, the Cruzans went into local probate court in their hometown of Carthage and asked Judge Robert E. Teel to authorize them to have the feeding tubes removed. William Colby, the Cruzan lawyer who donated his services to the family, later recalled that when he went before Judge Teel to make the request in the summer of 1988, he thought it would be a one-day hearing, since the law as expounded in other jurisdictions seemed to support the parents' acting as surrogate decision maker. Because of Nancy's incompetency, the court appointed a guardian, Thad C. McCanse, to represent her interests; at the initial hearing, he also sided with the family. Judge Teel heard the petition, asked some questions, and granted the request.

But Attorney General William L. Webster decided to appeal the case, and claimed that under Missouri law, there had to be clear and convincing evidence that Nancy Cruzan had earlier indicated that in such circumstances, she would want all medical assistance terminated. Although her parents had said this was her wish, Webster claimed that they had not met the burden of proof required under state law. The state, in its role as special guardian of incompetent persons, placed a high value on life. Webster did not dispute that people had the right to stop treatment; rather, he argued, the state had an equally compelling right to insist that there be clear evidence of the patient's wishes. In fact, in January 1990, Webster proposed legislation to the Missouri legislature to establish clear guidelines on who would be able to make decisions in cases like Nancy Cruzan's and what criteria should govern the decisions. Joe Cruzan immediately endorsed the proposal, saying, "It's just what we've been fighting for."

The Missouri Supreme Court, by a vote of 4 to 3, reversed Judge Teel and upheld the attorney general. The Cruzans appealed to the Supreme Court, which accepted the case and heard oral argument by the two sides in December 1989. The Court issued its decision the following July. Chief Justice William H. Rehnquist's opinion upheld the right to die, but balanced it against the state's interest in preserving life. While acknowledging that the Cruzans were "loving and caring parents," the Court regretfully rejected their plea.

In an extremely cautious opinion the majority ruled that there was indeed a right to die. Chief Justice Rehnquist, however, emphasized that this right did not derive from any constitutional guarantee of privacy, but from the Fourteenth Amendment's Due Process Clause: "The principle that a competent person has a constitutionally protected liberty interest in refusing unwanted medical treatment may be inferred from our prior decisions."

The key word is "competent," and the Court noted that this is an area normally assigned to state jurisdiction, not federal law.

Although only two other states, New York and Maine, require the same high level of proof as Missouri does, under a federal system a state's powerful interest in protecting life gives it the authority to establish such a test. Missouri law, the Chief Justice concluded, did not unduly burden the individual's constitutionally protected right to autonomy.

Perhaps the element of the majority opinion most disturbing to civil libertarians was the discussion of this balancing of an individual's liberty interest against the countervailing state concerns. Stating that a liberty interest exists merely begins the judicial inquiry; before a person can fully enjoy that interest, courts must determine whether the liberty interest outweighs the claims of the state. Rehnquist seemed to indicate that the courts should use little more than a "rational basis" test, the lowest standard of constitutional review, in weighing individual liberty interests in this area against state concerns. Thus, if the state can show a rational basis, such as the state's desire to preserve life, for depriving an individual of his or her liberty interest, the courts will, under *Cruzan,* uphold that state claim. Moreover, it places the burden of proof on the family of an incompetent to "prove" that the patient, if competent and able to make his or her wishes known, would want medical treatment or artificial feeding terminated. In those states with high evidentiary standards, this may be a difficult or even impossible demand.

That, of course, is what Missouri wanted—not that Nancy Cruzan should live forever as a vegetable, but that there be clear and convincing evidence that she would have chosen death in these circumstances. While it might appear that Missouri acted in a cruel and heartless manner, in fact it carried on a long and honorable tradition, that of the state legitimately seeking to protect the lives of its citizens, even the life of a person in a persistent vegetative state.

The wording of the minority opinion by Justice William H. Brennan indicates that it might have been written as a draft of a majority opinion and that Sandra Day O'Connor held the key vote. The four justices in the minority, Brennan, Thurgood

Marshall, Harry Blackmun, and John Paul Stevens, would have struck the balance more in favor of the individual than of the state. The Missouri rule, Brennan charged, "transforms human beings into passive subjects of medical technology," and in essence gives the final power to decide to the state and not to the individual. The majority decision, he claimed, "robs a patient of the very qualities protected by the right to avoid unwanted medical treatment. His own degraded existence is perpetuated; the memory he leaves behind becomes more and more distorted . . . [and] the idea of being remembered in their persistent vegetative state rather than as they were before their illness or accident may be very disturbing."

Despite the lengthy and numerous opinions, two things stand out in the decision. Most important, the Court for the first time formally acknowledged a right to die, and grounded it in the old common law notion of self-determination, or autonomy, as confirmed in the Due Process Clause. Second, the Court allowed Missouri to establish the "clear and convincing" rule of evidence, but did not require other states to adopt it. Too many people merely read in the headlines that the Cruzans had lost and jumped to the conclusion that there was no right to die or that people in Nancy Cruzan's condition had to be kept artificially alive for years, perhaps decades.

Even Justice Scalia, who was least sympathetic to the notion of a constitutionally protected right to die, agreed with the majority's ruling; his main concern seems to have been that these issues are primarily questions of state law and should not be decided in federal courts, a position that reflected his strongly held views regarding distribution of responsibility in a federal system. Justice O'Connor's concurrence almost shaded over into the Brennan view, and it appears that she was far more sympathetic to the idea than her colleagues in the majority. But she, too, has firm views on federalism, and urged that the rights of incompetents be worked out in "the laboratory" of the states.

Following the Supreme Court decision, Nancy Cruzan's parents went back into Judge Teel's probate court with "new" evidence, testimony from friends that Nancy had said she would never have wanted to be kept alive by machines or feeding tubes. William Webster, the state's attorney general, had won his legal point, but aware of the immense sympathy generated for the Cruzans, withdrew the state from the case. "The public sentiment has shifted," said Ronald E. Cranford, a neurologist who advised the family. "It's not politically advantageous to be against the Cruzan family anymore." George Annas agreed: "It's hard to find anyone who thinks that Nancy Cruzan should not be disconnected from the feeding tube."

Judge Teel heard the new evidence in early November 1990, and Thad McCanse, still acting as court-appointed guardian, also brought in evidence to support the Cruzans in their claim that disconnecting the feeding tube would be carrying out Nancy's wishes. On December 14, 1990, Judge Teel gave them what they had so long sought, and the hospital removed the feeding tube less than two hours later. It soon became apparent that not everyone shared Professor Annas's view. Nurses in the Missouri Rehabilitation Center hospital felt betrayed and angry at having to stop caring for the young woman who been their patient for nearly eight years. "The Humane Society won't let you starve your dog," said Sharon Orr, and another nurse noted that "they don't starve death row inmates." The head nurse of the unit, Jeanette Forsyth, bitterly attacked the decision and said, "We don't want her blood to be on our hands."

Protesters tried to get into the hospital, and when turned back by guards they mounted a prayer vigil outside, with signs demanding "Help Save Nancy!" and "How Would You Like to Be Starved to Death?" A group opposing euthanasia went to court seeking to overrule Judge Teel, but various state courts, the Missouri Supreme Court, and a federal district judge all denied their petitions. Mobile television units parked outside the hospital, while Nancy's family sat at her bedside. Twelve days after removal of the feeding tube, Nancy Beth Cruzan died quietly at 2:55 A.M. on the day after Christmas, 1990, unaware of the controversy that had swirled around her for so long.

The cases between 1974 and 1990 were, for the most part, the "easy" legal questions. Although different courts have adopted differing notions of how a right to die may be expressed and what its bases are, there is a clear line from Karen Quinlan to Nancy Cruzan: Competent patients, and lawful surrogates for incompetents who can show some evidence to support their interpretation of the patient's supposed wishes, may request the termination of medical treatment, even if that termination will result in their death. The harder cases were yet to come, and just as the legal questions would grow murkier, so too would the moral dimensions of the debate.

CHAPTER 4

Physicians and Assisted Suicide

The debate over physician-assisted suicide often begins—and ends—with the activities of Jack Kevorkian, the so-called Dr. Death who has reportedly assisted more than 130 people to end their lives. But the issues involved transcend the activities of the retired pathologist. He has pushed the envelope and offended many people, but he has also become a hero to those who believe that society ignores the needs and the wishes of those for whom life no longer has any value. Most important, Kevorkian has forced a public debate over the options people should have at the end of life.

On June 4, 1990, in a van parked in a public park outside Detroit, Dr. Jack Kevorkian hooked up what he called his "Mercy Machine" to 54-year-old Janet Adkins, a Portland, Oregon, schoolteacher suffering from the early stages of Alzheimer's disease. Ms. Adkins had read about Kevorkian, a longtime advocate of physician-assisted suicide, and she had contacted him in the fall of 1989. After some correspondence and phone calls, Kevorkian agreed to help her end her life, and Janet Adkins and her husband Ron flew east to meet with him. To make sure that she understood exactly what she was doing, Kevorkian set up a videocamera in a hotel room, and recorded a forty-minute conversation with the woman:

> KEVORKIAN: How was your life before, and how is it different now?
> ADKINS: My life was wonderful before, because I could play the piano. I could read. And I can't do any of those things. . . .

KEVORKIAN: Janet, you know what you're asking me to do?

ADKINS: Yes.

KEVORKIAN: You realize that. You want help from me. . . . You realize that I can make arrangements for everything, and you would have to do it. That you would have to push the button.

ADKINS: I understand.

KEVORKIAN: Janet, are you aware of your decision, and the implications of your decision?

ADKINS: Yes.

KEVORKIAN: What does it mean?

ADKINS: That I can get out with dignity.

The next morning, Kevorkian showed Janet Adkins his device, three vials suspended over a metal box containing a small electric motor. Once the doctor had inserted an intravenous tube into her arm, she could press a button that would start the flow of saline solution; then it would open the valve to the second vial, releasing thiopental, which would induce unconsciousness; finally, the contents of the third vial, potassium chloride, would cause her heart to stop.

Kevorkian again asked Janet Adkins if she understood what would happen, if she wanted to go ahead, if she knew what to do. She assured him she did. Kevorkian attached an electrocardiograph and left the van; when he came back a little while later, Ms. Adkins was dead. The retired pathologist then called the police and reported the death.

The story of "Dr. Death," as the media soon labeled him, exploded all over the nation's newspapers and television stations. Doctors, ethicists, and laypeople alike all had something to say, and so did the law. Oakland County assistant prosecutor Michael Modelsky sought a first-degree murder charge, but after a two-day preliminary hearing, Judge Gerald McNally ruled that the state had failed to prove that Kevorkian had planned and carried out the death of the woman. Ms. Adkins, McNally noted, had caused her own death, and since Michigan had no prohibition against assisting in a suicide, Kevorkian had broken no law. But obviously appalled at the event, McNally called upon the state legislature to address the issue.

Then in January 1991, Modelsky filed a civil suit to stop Kevorkian from using his device in the future. The four-day trial heard testimony from doctors, who denounced Kevorkian for violating medical ethics, as well as from people who praised the "Mercy Machine" and wanted the legal opportunity to use it. Dr. Arthur Caplan, of the University of Minnesota Center for Biomedical Ethics, said Kevorkian's actions fell "well outside acceptable practice for physicians" and that they would undermine the public's view of "doctors as people they can trust, who will not abuse their power and take life unnecessarily." Actually, opinion within medical circles seemed to be split on the case. Although many doctors criticized Kevorkian's handling of the Adkins situation, they did not necessarily disapprove of his intent. A survey by the New York–based *Medical Tribune* found about 45 percent approved of Kevorkian's actions.

To defend Dr. Kevorkian's actions as humane and compassionate, defense attorney Geoffrey Fieger called Sherry Miller to the stand. Mrs. Miller, the 42–year-old mother of two teenagers, had been battling the crippling effects of multiple sclerosis for more than a dozen years, and she could not even lift her hand to take the oath. She described the ravages of the disease: "I went from a cane to a walker to a wheelchair. I can't walk. I can't write. . . . I can't function as a human being. What can anybody do? Nothing. I want the right to die." Medical science had been unable to help her, and Kevorkian's machine now seemed her only hope. "I should have done something sooner when I was more—when I was capable of doing something on my own." When asked if she could not do something on her own now, Ms. Miller said no. "I can't take a bunch of pills because I can't get to them," and she did not have the strength or the coordination to use a gun.

The attorney then asked what she thought of the statements by some of the medical ethicists who had testified that people who are in pain or have terminal illnesses can be made more comfortable through medical treatment, so there is no need to end their lives. "You sit in this chair for a year," she said, "not being able to do anything, and being made comfortable, and then tell me. You know, the quality of life after you sit in here—in my chair."

The defense called other witnesses who related how Kevorkian's machine offered them their only hope out of a nightmarish situation. Virginia Bernero told of her son Victor's four-year battle with AIDS, and his great pain and suffering. They saw a story about Kevorkian on television, and Victor said he wanted to use the machine. Victor had died in November 1990, and his family said he suffered needlessly; to them, as her other son, Virgil, said, Kevorkian is "a hero and a trailblazer in a field of processionary caterpillars."

———

Although a Michigan lawmaker had promised to introduce legislation to govern such cases, Judge Alice Gilbert had no statute in place to guide her decision. But law libraries are far from devoid of information and cases dealing with aiding, abetting, or counseling suicide. Under common law, if one counseled another to commit suicide, that person could be held guilty of aiding and abetting murder. If present at the time of the actual death, the adviser could be charged as a principal in the second degree; if not present, then he or she in all likelihood would go free, even though technically an accessory before the fact. The reason the adviser would escape punishment lies in the common law rule that an accessory cannot be tried for a crime unless the perpetrator has been convicted, and obviously, one cannot try a successful suicide.

The great English jurist Blackstone believed, however, that "if one persuades another to kill himself, and he does so, the advisor is guilty of murder," and a few states have adopted that view. Also, in so-called suicide pacts, if two persons agree to kill themselves together and only one dies, the survivor is considered guilty of the murder of the one who dies.

In a federal system such as ours, it is possible for events that are legal—or at least noncriminal—in one state to be outlawed in another. Jack Kevorkian escaped criminal charges because

Michigan had no statute addressing assisted suicide, but had he set up his machine in Missouri or Oregon he might well have been indicted and convicted as an accessory to murder.

Judge Gilbert eventually issued an injunction against Kevorkian's using the machine to help other people commit suicide. "His goal is self-service rather than patient service," she charged, and his fellow physicians "look upon him as a menace that threatens the existence of the medical profession." Although Kevorkian pronounced himself saddened by the ruling, he initially promised to abide by it, although "I can still speak out and promulgate ideas." One day later, however, he was counseling a cancer-stricken dentist about suicide and announcing that he would test the limits of the injunction. Then, in October 1991, as one news magazine put it, "Dr. Death Strikes Again."

One can hardly describe the two women involved as "murder victims." If anything, they saw themselves victimized by cruel diseases and a society that denied them the one release they sought. Marjorie Wantz, 58, suffered from a painful pelvic disorder; she had endured ten operations, none of which had helped, and had been housebound for more than three years. Neighbors said that her cries of pain could often be heard at night. She had met Kevorkian on a Detroit talk show and then had read the surprising runaway best-seller *Final Exit,* a how-to-do-it suicide manual by Hemlock Society founder Derek Humphry. She had tried to follow the instructions in the book and had failed; so she turned to Kevorkian and his machine. The other woman, Sherry Miller, 43, had testified at Kevorkian's trial; she did not have the strength left even to push the button, so Kevorkian arranged for her to breathe carbon monoxide through a mask, while her best friend sat at her side. Kevorkian was present at the cabin in Bald Mountain Park, about forty miles north of Detroit, and after both women had died, he called the police. When the county sheriff arrived, the bodies were still hooked up to the machines. Kevorkian's lawyer, Geoffrey Fieger, noted that his client "provided the expertise. He provided the equipment." Asked whether he expected Kevorkian to be prosecuted, Fieger said "No . . . it's a humane, ethical, medical act."

Kevorkian remained free of criminal charges; the state assembly, despite the extensive publicity surrounding the death of Janet Adkins, had failed to enact any legislation on assisted suicide. Prosecutors tried to indict him on murder charges for assisting Marjorie Wantz and Sherry Miller to commit suicide, but failed. When they did manage to bring him to trial on a later indictment, the jury refused to convict. Eventually Michigan prosecutors gave up, recognizing that even if they could secure a grand jury indictment, petit juries would not convict him. Whatever moral judgment one wishes to make about his behavior, he did not violate Michigan law as it then stood.

Kevorkian's case is unique in that he sees himself as an advocate and seeks publicity for his cause. The fact of the matter is that doctors assist their patients to commit suicide every day of the year. Most of them do so quietly and indirectly, with perhaps only the family knowing or guessing the truth. The columnist Anna Quindlen recalled a conversation she had once had with a friend whose mother suffered from the pain of ovarian cancer. Her friend spoke of the wonderful oncologist treating her mother, and how kind and patient and considerate he was, but those were not his greatest virtue. "He told me how many of my mother's painkillers constituted a lethal dose."

Many doctors admit that the rate of suicide among the elderly is far higher than the statistics indicate, and the known suicide rate is twice that of younger groups. Elderly people often are prescribed powerful medicines, which if taken improperly can cause death; the warnings indicating what is improper use can also serve as a guide to suicide.

One doctor, speaking anonymously, said, "So the sick old man dies at home in his own bed last night instead of next fall in some intensive care unit. He was in pain. He was suffering a lot. What good would come from an autopsy that finds some lethal dose? I'm not suspicious of the family. So I sign the death certificate for 'natural causes'." Another doctor, who had treated more than four hundred AIDS patients, told each of them that whenever they thought treatment or pain had become too much, he would provide medicine for a painless suicide. Only four accepted his offer, but he reported that they all felt that they had regained some control over their lives. In 1989, when the doctor himself developed AIDS, he took his own prescription, and his death certificate did not list suicide.

Doctors are sworn to protect life, but far more than most people in society, they see death. They see people so diseased and wracked with pain that death is preferable to life, and they are unique in having the power and the resources to bring that release. Although some newspapers condemned Kevorkian for "disgracing" the medical profession, doctors may, both legally and ethically, help patients to die.

The doctor who agrees to forgo treatment, or to help patients avoid further treatment, is not assisting in suicide. Courts have consistently ruled that forgoing treatment is not suicide, because the act of refusing treatment is not the cause of death; people die from their illness, not from withdrawal of treatment. Suicide is self-inflicted death; the illness that leads to death is not self-inflicted.

To some people, this appears as sophistry, the drawing of fine lines to disguise or rationalize murder. But the law is made of fine distinctions, not just in the criminal area but in civil law as well. One has to take into account the facts of the situation, the motives of the actors, the rights of both society and the individual. Nor is the law immune from morality or compassion, and that is as it ought to be.

Courts also consider intent in distinguishing forgoing treatment from committing suicide. In suicide the person's specific wish is to die, while patients declining treatment do not necessarily wish to die so much as relieve their suffering. One can find this most clearly stated in the case of Abe Perlmutter, a victim of Lou Gehrig's disease who petitioned the court to have his respirator removed. The court noted that Perlmutter's testimony showed "he really wants to live, but to do so, God and Mother Nature willing, under his own power. The basic wish to live, plus the fact that he did not self-induce his horrible affliction, precludes his further refusal of treatment being classified as attempted suicide."

———

Because doctors can help their patients die as well as live, it is not surprising that people turn to them for assistance. Some doctors are affronted by such requests; they have sworn to heal people, not to kill them, and they refuse to be accessories to suicide because of their own deeply felt moral convictions. On the other hand, many doctors will in one way or another quietly assist their patients to commit suicide. Shortly after the Kevorkian story broke, one doctor came forward and admitted that he had done just that.

Dr. Timothy Quill practices medicine in upstate Rochester, New York. In March 1991 he did what no doctor had done before, publicly discuss his role in assisting a patient to commit suicide, and he did so in an article in the prestigious *New England Journal of Medicine.* Quill had known his patient, whom he called "Diane," for eight years, and had watched her as she had overcome alcoholism and depression and begin to enjoy life. Then she fell ill, and Quill diagnosed her ailment as acute leukemia. "Together we lamented her tragedy and the unfairness of life," but he urged her to start chemotherapy as soon as possible, after which she would have a bone marrow transplant. Quill also told Diane that the bone marrow treatment would be painful and that at best it offered a one-in-four chance of survival.

Diane refused the treatment. She was convinced, she told Quill, that she would die during the treatment and would suffer unspeakably in the process. "There was no way I could say this would not occur," he recalled. "In fact, the last four patients with acute leukemia at our hospital had died very painful deaths."

Aware that her death would be only a matter of time, Diane came around to the idea of suicide, and asked Quill to prescribe something that would end her life with as little pain as possible when the time came. Quill discussed the matter with her, but initially would not agree. He referred her to the Hemlock Society, and a week later she called and asked him for a prescription for barbiturates—sleeping pills—because she was having trouble sleeping. The doctor knew this to be true, but he also recognized that if she had the pills, she would have some security, some control over her life, and could thus live the weeks or months left to her without fear of a lingering and painful death. So he wrote the prescription. "I made sure that she knew how to use the barbiturates for sleep and also that she knew the amount needed to commit suicide."

Diane's condition grew worse. She made her farewells to family and friends and asked Quill to come over to say good-bye. Two days later her husband called to say that Diane had died quietly on the couch; Quill reported the cause of death as acute leukemia. It was the truth, but not the whole truth, and he did it to protect both the family and himself from investigation and possible prosecution for assisting in suicide.

Up until this point, the story of Dr. Quill and his patient is similar to hundreds, perhaps thousands, that occur in the United States every year. But then Timothy Quill decided to talk about it, in part to relieve the intense emotional stress the experience had produced, but also to lift the lid on a widespread practice, bring it into the open, and make it more honest. As he later told a reporter, "There's an elephant in the room, and nobody's talking about it because they don't want to deal with the darker side of illness."

Quill consulted with attorneys for New York State before deciding to publish his account, and was told he probably would not face prosecution. While Quill prescribed the barbiturates, he had done so for legitimate reasons, and Diane had taken the overdose by her own hand. Because assisting a suicide is a felony in New York, punishable by a five- to fifteen-year prison sentence, local prosecutors did bring the case to a Rochester grand jury, but the jurors refused to indict Quill.

Medical ethicists Arthur Caplan and George Annas, both of whom criticized Kevorkian, found Timothy Quill's case altogether different. Annas put it quite simply: "I want this guy as my doctor. The vast majority of people . . . would want somebody like this." (Polls taken within the last few years find that out of every ten American adults, five to seven believe that people suffering from incurable disease should be allowed to commit suicide.) Kevorkian, Caplan explained, worked with someone he barely knew and was not medically competent to make a judgment of her mental condition or even of the progress of her illness. Diane's situation was completely different, and Quill did nothing wrong.

> He knew his patient. I think he felt he could not control her pain anymore. He knew that she was terminally ill. And in a sense, all he did was provide her with the means to activate a choice, but it was her responsibility to decide when and if to use the drugs that she ultimately did use to take her life. The doctor in this case behaved in a very ethical manner.

One could argue with the distinctions Caplan draws; both Quill and Kevorkian knew that the actions they took would have particular consequences. If Kevorkian had prescribed pills and then left Janet Adkins to take them, would that have been more ethical or humane? Possibly, once hooked up to the "Mercy Machine," Janet Adkins might have felt pressure to go ahead, but by all accounts she had been the one to approach Kevorkian. She had already decided to end her life. Not everyone has a loving, caring family member or spouse to help them die. Should doctors, who have the knowledge and training in this area, be allowed to ease their patients out of life?

————

Doctors, medical ethicists, and politicians are widely split over the issue of physician-assisted suicide. The general public, at least according to polls, seems to favor the idea, although there are significant groups opposed. It is a public policy issue of great moment, and we as a nation are going through an important debate over the merits of allowing doctors to assist their patients, not just to die peacefully, but to actively end their lives.

If one reads the pages of the official medical organization journals or listens to testimony before legislative committees, one would think that doctors overwhelmingly oppose physician-assisted suicide. Historically the role of doctors has been to save life and to ease pain. The Hippocratic oath specifically abjures helping patients kill themselves—"I will give no deadly medicines to any one if asked, nor suggest any such counsel." But from the time of Hippocrates down until this century, doctors have had limited tools with which to work. They had some potions that could ease pain, reduce swelling, and give limited relief to other forms of illness. If they did not actively help their patients to die, many did so indirectly. And there is some evidence that doctors often took matters into their own hands to ease suffering.

In January 1988 the *Journal of the American Medical Association* published an article entitled "It's Over, Debbie," in which an anonymous gynecology resident at a large unnamed city hospital told of deliberately administering a lethal dose of morphine to end the suffering of a young woman named Debbie, who was in the last stages of ovarian cancer. The story, which some commentators believed to be untrue, nonetheless triggered a firestorm of protest within the profession. Doctors and ethicists condemned the injection as unethical and unprincipled, as murder, a violation of all that doctors are supposed to hold dear.

This event, predating by more than two years Janet Adkins's suicide with the help of Jack Kevorkian, set the American Medical Association (AMA) and its related state and local medical societies on a path from which it has never deviated—absolute opposition to the legalization of physician-assisted suicide. The AMA position is concerned less with the rights of patients than it is with the integrity of the profession, but so long as the medical societies formally oppose assisted suicide, there is little chance that state assemblies will push through enabling legislation over their resistance.

The essence of the AMA position is simple—"Doctors Must Not Kill." As Dr. Willard Gaylin wrote in response to the Debbie article, "Generations of physicians and commentators on medical ethics have underscored and held fast to the distinction between ceasing useless treatments (or allowing to die) and active, willful taking of life; at least since the Oath of Hippocrates,

Western medicine has regarded the killing of patients, even on request, as a profound violation of the deepest meaning of the medical vocation." Gaylin went on to aver that the issue of physician-assisted suicide "touches medicine at its very moral center; if this moral center collapses, if physicians become killers or are even merely licensed to kill, the profession—and therewith each physician—will never again be worthy of trust and respect as healer and comforter and protector of life."

What Gaylin and others worry about is that if doctors are allowed to openly help patients end their lives—through either prescribing lethal drugs or actually administering them—then one of the basic foundations of the doctor-patient relationship, the trust between the two, will be destroyed. Patients will no longer know whether they are receiving care that will cure them or kill them, especially if they are elderly, infirm, or suffering from an incurable illness. They will no longer trust their doctors nor be honest in describing their symptoms, for fear that doctors will opt for death rather than life.

The official medical groups have unwaveringly stuck to this position. In 1995 Kirk Johnson, the general counsel to the AMA, wrote to the attorney general of Michigan to offer the AMA's full assistance in any prosecution of Jack Kevorkian. Citing the AMA Code of Ethics, Johnson declared physician-assisted suicide "simply incompatible with the physician's role as healer. When faced with patients who are terminally ill and suffering, physicians must relieve their suffering by providing adequate comfort care." In an *amicus* brief filed with the Supreme Court in the assisted suicide cases, the AMA joined the American Psychiatric Association and other health providers in opposing any form of legalized suicide assistance.

The AMA response appears, on first blush, an overreaction. Because a doctor is capable of administering lethal doses does not necessarily mean that she will. Surely there is a middle ground between the action of the nameless resident who on his own decided to end Debbie's life and the absolute refusal to end a patient's suffering by prescribing painkillers that might, if taken in too great a quantity, lead to death. There is, but it is a ground that doctors prefer not to discuss openly.

In presentations to legislatures and in briefs to courts, medical associations have offered palliative care as an alternative to assisted suicide. Assuming that it is pain that leads many incurably ill people to seek death, the medical profession offers pain management, the use of drugs to alleviate suffering. While this certainly seems to make sense, the fact is that when pain reaches a certain level, the amount of morphine (the drug of choice in pain relief for terminally ill patients) necessary to stop the pain reaches a lethal level.

The medical profession is comfortable with this so-called double effect of palliative care and sees it as an acceptable practice, one condoned by doctors, courts, hospitals, and, quite often, families. A patient who is terminally ill and in pain is put on a morphine drip, with the amount of medication proportional to the level of pain. As the pain increases, so will the dosage. At some point, however, the quantity of morphine will be so great that it will depress the ability of the body to breathe and will lead to a quiet and painless death. Although the proximate cause of death will, in fact, be morphine overdose, the certificate will invariably ascribe death to the underlying illness.

In interviews, many doctors indicate they prefer not having physician-assisted suicide legalized. Such legalization would require regulation, and doctors believe there is already far too much regulation of medicine. But on a practical basis, they argue that what patients want is an end to suffering and that morphine and other drugs provide it. For those who prefer death, that too is available, though not in the simple form of one lethal overdose. Doctors indicate they believe that providing pain relief, even if it leads to death, is compatible with their oaths as physicians; prescribing or administering lethal injections is not.

Many doctors, however, disagree with the official position of the AMA (to which only 40 percent of American doctors belong), and other groups have begun to take differing positions. Some, such as "Physicians against Euthanasia, Assisted Suicide and Withdrawal of Nutrition" take an even stronger pro-life stance. Thomas Preston, a cardiologist at the University of Washington, condemns morphine drips as just another name for euthanasia, and is quite blunt—and correct—when he claims that approval of palliative care with its double effect says to physicians, "Practice [euthansia] covertly, and you will be all right."

The Hemlock Society has provided a forum for doctors who wish to openly oppose the AMA position. The American Medical Student Association and the American Medical Women's Association both support physician-assisted suicide, and the former group filed an *amicus* brief with the Supreme Court in the suicide cases. In Washington and Oregon, where pro–assisted suicide groups managed to get the issue onto a ballot (see next chapter), polls show doctors split about evenly on the issue, while the medical societies strongly opposed the measures.

National and local surveys also show a large number of doctors who differ with the AMA. Studies of oncologists and other specialists dealing with terminally ill patients indicate strong support for physician-assisted suicide, and some studies indicate that 15 percent or more of American doctors have, in fact, helped their patients to die.

Perhaps doctors who have to deal with terminally ill patients every day have a greater empathy for those who want to have some control over their end-of-life decisions. An oncologist at the Medical College of Virginia tells his patients that he will do everything possible to get them into remission and to alleviate their pain. But, he says, if the cancer does not respond to treatment, if the pain becomes unbearable, he will also provide them with a lethal overdose of medication, help them to take it, and stay with them until the end.

Timothy Quill, who in some ways opened the Pandora's box, has in the last decade become an ardent advocate of physician-assisted suicide, although he shies away from the Kevorkian model. Prohibition of physician-assisted suicide, he argues, "handcuffs doctors who want to show compassion to patients whose bodies are irreversibly falling apart." His writings are sensitive not only to the needs of patients, but also to the burdens placed upon doctors. The doctor needs to be aware not only of the physical but also of the emotional and spiritual suffering of his patients, and this can be a heavy burden. Nonetheless, for doctors to provide compassionate care at the end of life, they must go beyond the medical model they learned in school.

Among health care providers who oppose physician-assisted suicide are doctors who believe that pain management always provides a better option for patients than death and advocates of hospice care for the terminally ill. The two are closely related, because the main function of hospice care is to manage and ease the pain of the dying.

David Cundiff, an oncologist and hospice care physician, strongly opposes physician-assisted suicide and argues that people should be allowed to die naturally, their pain eased by appropriate medication. The hospice approach seeks to relieve the physical suffering of the patients and also provides psychological support for both the patient and the family. He notes that where the standard medical treatment for cancer or AIDS is to fight the disease aggressively and to prolong life at virtually any cost, the hospice "seeks to optimize the quality of life of the patient's remaining time." The National Hospice Organization defines this philosophy as follows:

> Hospice affirms life. Hospice exists to provide support and care for persons in the last phases of incurable disease so that they might live as fully and comfortably as possible. Hospice recognizes dying as a normal process whether or not resulting from disease. Hospice neither hastens nor postpones death. Hospice exists in the hope and belief that, through appropriate care and the promotion of a caring community sensitive to their needs, patients and families may be free to attain a degree of mental and spiritual preparation for death that is satisfactory to them.

The problem, as even the most ardent hospice advocates recognize, is that hospice care in the United States is terribly inadequate. Even if everyone suffering from a terminal illness who wanted to commit suicide agreed to go to a hospice, there would be enough beds to handle only a fraction of them.

The medical theory underlying hospice care is palliation, the relief of pain. Many hospice champions as well as other doctors argue that people do not really want to commit suicide; they want either to be free from pain or to reduce it to bearable levels. Kathleen Foley, a neurologist, claims that "it's a well documented fact that those asking for assisted suicide almost always change their minds once we have their pain under control." To Foley, who has been a pioneering advocate of pain management for a number of years, American doctors are poorly trained in this area. "Even oncology residents and fellows are poorly trained. People are crying out in agony. We are not listening to them."

A good example of how poorly understood pain management is occurred in McLean, Virginia, in the spring of 1996. Dr. William E. Hurwitz, a nationally known Washington, D.C., pain specialist, prescribed massive doses of narcotics for some of his patients. Many pharmacies do not carry large amounts of such drugs, which are controlled substances closely regulated by law, but Jerome A. Danoff, who owned a small independent pharmacy, agreed to stock the amounts to fill Dr. Hurwitz's prescriptions and even agreed to mail the medication to out-of-state patients. After one of Hurwitz's patients died of a drug overdose, the Virginia Department of Health Professions summarily suspended Hurwitz's medical license and Danoff's pharmaceutical license. In the end, a public outcry from Hurwitz's patients, who told the press as well as legislative hearings about the pain they suffered and the medication that was the only thing that made life bearable, forced the regulatory boards to back down and reinstate the two men's licenses.

There is no question that when pain can be controlled, people are less interested in dying. But there are other issues, which Foley and other pain-management advocates ignore. Often, to alleviate intense pain, the level of morphine, hydromorphine, or methadone is so high as to dull the patient's senses. There are several steps in palliative care. Initially, strong medication can relieve the suffering without impairing the patient's mental alertness. But as the body either builds up resistance to the drug or the illness progresses, the level of medication has to be increased. My aunt died in a hospice, and at the end she was unconscious most of the day, free from pain but also totally unaware of her existence. And, of course, if one raises the morphine drip high enough, death results.

Not everyone agrees with the view that if pain can be managed, then people will not want to commit suicide. In a study done in Holland, where physician-assisted suicide is permissible, studies seem to indicate that pain is not the main reason people seek to end their lives. They talk about loss of control or a deterioration in the quality of their lives. It is this aspect of illness and old age that many opponents of physician-assisted suicide either ignore or dismiss out of hand.

The opposition to physician-assisted suicide is not limited to religious groups or some segments of the health care community. Within the community of medical ethicists there is a long, loud, and ongoing debate about physician-assisted suicide. Just as Tom Beauchamp and James Childress support it as a legitimate expression of individual autonomy, so Daniel Callahan has argued against it for more than thirty years; his views predate the Quinlan case, which brought the issue of euthanasia to the fore, and they have remained consistent through all this time.

Callahan is the cofounder and president of the Hasting Institute, a research organization located in suburban New York that specializes in biomedical ethics. The debate, he claims, is not only about medicine, but more important, about what we want to be as a people. Americans, he concedes, are highly and proudly individualistic, but that individualism can cut more ways than one. "Today we no longer have confidence that we will be taken care of once we are weakened and no longer able to assert control by the pure force of our wills. What we are trying to do with assisted suicide is to take a step beyond which there are no other steps in gaining full individual self-determination."

People have always committed suicide, and society, while never maintaining that self-murder is good, looked on these cases as sad, but forgivable. In his influential 1993 book, *The Troubled Dream of Life: In Search of a Peaceful Death*, Callahan wrote:

> With physician-assisted suicide, we have a sea change: we are saying it is good, humane, and dignified and that it can be handled in some systematic way, free from abuse. But under this guise of a new-found empathy, it will be no more than an exercise in self-deception, a societal deceit, with a medical cover-up. And if this is humane, it will become a legitimate medical option.

People will now find doctors telling them that they can prescribe expensive, painful, and ultimately futile treatments, or they can help you die, and the pressure on the elderly and the infirm will be unbearable. There are, Callahan concedes, cases where termination of life may be merciful, but these are always the exception and should never be made the rule.

Callahan's views are informed not only by reverence for individual life, but also by his fears of what legitimizing physician-assisted suicide might do to society. In his view it would devalue human life and lead people to seek escape from the trials and tribulations that make life meaningful. "We are not fully formed people without going through these life crises."

As to individual autonomy, Callahan has for many years dismissed it as overrated. People cannot do whatever they want as individuals, because they are also members of a community. In a complex world, the value of an individual life is important as part of the building blocks and stability of society. Devalue life, he warns, and you will destroy society.

Other medical ethicists, as well as Callahan, worry about the effect of physician-assisted suicide on doctors and the medical profession. In an *amicus* brief filed with the Supreme Court, several bioethics professors, including George Annas, argued that not only was assisted suicide not a recognized medical procedure, but legitimizing it would undermine the doctor-patient relationship. Unlike abortion, which they claimed is performed in the "context of a confidential physician-patient relationship without direct state or third party interference or review," physician-assisted suicide would require massive governmental regulation. The level of trust between doctor and patient, built upon the bedrock of confidentiality and freedom from outside interference, would be destroyed. Ironically, the *amicus* brief looked to the very safeguards built into the Oregon scheme (see next chapter) to prevent abuse as proof of the heavy-handed government regulation that any scheme of physician-assisted suicide would require.

Two other centers of opposition should be briefly noted. Antiabortion groups have consistently opposed not only physician-assisted suicide, but in many cases any form of euthanasia, even passive. For them the argument is the same in both cases—life is a precious God-given gift, and to deny it, through either abortion of the unborn or murder, even self-murder, is an affront to God. The two are linked, in Pope John Paul II's term, in a "culture of death."

Another group opposing physician-assisted suicide consists of some people with disabilities, who, recalling the example of Nazi Germany, fear a slippery slope in which it is one or two small steps from euthanizing people at their own request to doing away with others who are considered drags on society, such as the elderly, the ill, and the disabled. One of the most vociferous opponents of physician-assisted suicide is a group calling itself "Not Dead Yet." On the day the Supreme Court heard oral argument in the assisted suicide cases, members of Not Dead Yet mounted a picket line in front of the Court, rolling around in their wheelchairs with signs proclaiming their love of life and the fact that they were "not dead yet." The group also maintains a website dedicated to fighting assisted suicide. Its motto is "Americans with Disabilities don't want your pity *or* your lethal mercy. We want freedom. We want LIFE."

On Sunday evening, November 22, the prime time news show *60 Minutes* carried a feature unlike any in the program's history. Millions of viewers watched as Mike Wallace aired an edited film clip of Jack Kevorkian administering a lethal dose of medication to Thomas Youk, 52, who suffered from Lou Gehrig's disease and who wanted to die on his own terms before the disease had so progressed that he would choke to death. In an interview with Kevorkian after the tape had been shown, the doctor admitted he was pushing the envelope, trying to get Americans to face up to the issue that tens of thousands of people were suffering needlessly and that if they desired, they ought to be allowed to die with the help of a doctor. The courts had fooled around long enough on side issues; Kevorkian had presented the legal system with a clear-cut case of a doctor's actually helping a patient die. Either he would win in the ensuing trial, or he would die in prison. In a particularly revealing admission, Kevorkian said that what he had done was in part for himself. He was now 70 years old, he told Wallace, and as a doctor he knew that his body would not go on forever. If he contracted a fatal illness or his mental and physical powers began to deteriorate, he wanted one of his colleagues to able to do—legally—what he had done for Youk.

The segment gave ammunition to both sides of the debate. Faye Girsh, executive director of the Hemlock Society USA, declared that Youk "was a very ill man dying a gentle, peaceful death in the time and manner he requested. . . . I think we should see more people dying this way." Opponents, of course, were horrified. "I certainly didn't see any compassion," raged Ned McGrath, spokesman for the Roman Catholic Archdiocese of Detroit. "His last minute on earth, and he's left in a room with Jack Kevorkian and a video camera. What a horrible way to leave the world." (Youk's family, which strongly supported his wishes and Kevorkian's action, was deliberately sent out of the room so the members could not be charged as accessories to any crime.)

Kevorkian did not have long to wait for his answer. After reviewing the entire tape, which CBS made available, Oakland

County (Michigan) prosecutor David Gorcyca filed first-degree murder charges against Kevorkian. Although Gorcyca asked that bail be denied, the judge released Kevorkian but warned him against participating in any further homicides. "Your honor, there won't be a parking ticket."

Kevorkian, for reasons known only to himself, chose to act as his own attorney, and did a terrible job of it. He clearly did not know the law, and the judge had to prompt him constantly. He wanted to bring Youk's family on as witnesses to prove that all he had done was carry out a patient's wishes. A good lawyer ought to have been able to get them on the stand, but Kevorkian could not. The judge ruled that in a murder trial, unlike in Kevorkian's previous four trials for assisted suicide, the consent of the deceased is irrelevant. Kevorkian did not deny what he had done, and the jury could see it all on tape. So after assisting in 130 suicides since 1990, Jack Kevorkian finally had no room left. In early April 1999, the jury found him guilty of second-degree murder, rather than the first-degree finding that the prosecutor had demanded. A week later Judge Jessica Cooper sentenced Kevorkian to prison for ten to twenty-five years. "Sir," she told him, "consider yourself stopped."

There will, undoubtedly, be an appeal, but it is doubtful if an appellate court will overturn the verdict. As Judge Cooper noted, "This trial was not about the political or moral correctness of euthanasia. It was about you, sir. It was about lawlessness. It was about disrespect for a society that exists because of the strength of the legal system. No one, sir, is above the law."

———

A few days after Kevorkian's conviction, Blackie Sherrod, a columnist for the *Dallas Morning News,* wrote about his grandfather, whom everyone called Uncle Dick. He had been a farmer until a combination of economic depression and drought drove him off the land. He then taught himself how to be a carpenter, and soon he was working again steadily in the little town to which he and his family had moved after they lost the farm. "He built everything in the little town: houses, barns, garages, and sheds. He replaced roofs and remodeled old homes. Name it, Uncle Dick built it." He worked hard well into his seventies, and after that contented himself with building desks, chairs, chests, and other pieces of furniture as gifts for friends and kin.

Then he suffered a stroke that took away movement in both legs and an arm. After that he lived in a hospital bed set up in his daughter's spare bedroom, tended to by family and a practical nurse who bathed and shaved him and took care of other things that this independent man had so long done for himself. Sherrod concludes: "Uncle Dick so passed his 91st birthday, silent and helplessly scourged to his dungeon. And had there, perchance, come a knock on the front door and there stood Dr. Jack Kevorkian, we would have baked him a cake, and my grandfather, could he have managed, would have crawled to the grocery to fetch the flour and eggs."

One can, as many people do, dismiss Kevorkian as a self-publicizing charlatan, or see him as the man who can end their pain in the world. But nearly everyone agrees that Jack Kevorkian has forced the American people to meet head-on the issue of physician-assisted suicide and to consider what can be done for ending the pain and humiliation and suffering of people like Sherrod's grandfather.

CHAPTER 5

Making Physician-Assisted Suicide Legal

In 1973 Dr. Geertruida Postma, a general practitioner in the Netherlands, stood trial for the murder of her mother by injection of morphine. The old lady lived in a nursing home, had suffered a cerebral hemorrhage that left her partially paralyzed, was deaf and spoke with great difficulty, and at the time was being treated for pneumonia. She had failed in a suicide attempt, and told her daughter, "I want to leave this life. Please help." At her trial Dr. Postma declared that she regretted not having done it earlier. The court found her guilty, and sentenced her to one week in jail and one year of probation.

Perhaps even more important, the court laid down guidelines under which assisted suicide would not be liable to criminal sanction. These conditions required that the patient be suffering from a terminal illness, be in unbearable pain, make a written request to the doctor, and have entered into "the dying phase" and that the assistance must be by a doctor, not a layperson. The case brought forth an outpouring of statements from other physicians that they would have done the same thing, and started the Netherlands down a path to becoming the only nation in the world where euthanasia, while technically illegal, could be practiced openly.

The Dutch experience has been used by both sides in the assisted suicide debate to reinforce their points. Supporters point to the small number of deaths resulting from physician action, while opponents declare that the practice has grown out of control, with many people involuntarily dying at the hands of doctors. One needs to understand how euthanasia works in the Netherlands, but one also needs to keep in mind that the United

States is a far different country, and it is questionable whether one can actually apply the Dutch experience to the American environment.

Nearly all analyses of the Dutch experience start with World War II, when the Germans occupied Holland for nearly five years. The Nazi satraps ordered the local doctors to help carry out their policies of sterilizing Jews, euthanizing the handicapped, and deporting Jews and other "undesirables" to labor camps. Alone of all the occupied countries, the Dutch medical profession as a group refused to participate in the Nazi atrocities. As a result the Germans voided all of the Dutch medical licenses, but the doctors continued to treat patients while no longer signing birth and death certificates. To force compliance the Nazis arrested one hundred doctors and deported them to labor camps in Germany, but the Dutch held firm and refused to collaborate; eventually the occupiers gave up. As a result of this experience, no one in Holland considers the doctors butchers or murderers, and charges of physicians "playing God" with patients' lives are pretty much absent from the Dutch debate (although not from the charges of those outside the Netherlands who condemn euthanasia).

Following the *Postma* decision, over the next twenty years a series of court rulings helped to refine what might be called the "unofficial" policy regarding physician-assisted suicide in the Netherlands, since technically the Dutch penal code still considers euthanasia a crime. Most of these cases came to the court in an effort more to develop a policy than to punish individual doctors. In this sense they resemble the collusive cases brought by hospitals and doctors in the United States to develop a legally sanctioned policy of allowing patients to terminate life support.

The crucial case involved a physician who had, at her request, helped a very sick and elderly woman to die. The case went all the way to the Supreme Court, which in 1984 sent it back to the Rotterdam local court for a rehearing. There the judges enunciated the so-called Rotterdam criteria, which narrowed the circumstances under which physician-assisted suicide would be permissible: the patient's death may not cause unnecessary suffering for others; following a patient's request the physician must consult the patient's family, unless the patient objects; and a second doctor has to agree with the prognosis.

That same year the Royal Dutch Medical Society announced its approval of physician-assisted dying and set out "Rules of Careful Conduct" to guide doctors. The Rotterdam criteria and the blessing of the organized professional body created a climate in which doctors could help end the lives of their patients without fear of prosecution. But a critical ingredient went missing. Under the guidelines doctors had to turn in extensive reports about the circumstances of deaths they aided and stand ready to be interviewed by an investigator from the Ministry of Justice if anything seemed out of the ordinary. As busy men and women, doctors often avoided the lengthy paperwork by signing death certificates listing the underlying cause of death, such as cancer, and neglecting to add that the death had been hastened by drugs.

As a result, the Ministry of Justice initially received only about a dozen reports a year of euthanasia, although the number increased as physicians grew more familiar with the practice. Because of conflicting information, the Dutch government in 1990 named a special commission headed by Professor Jan Remmelink, the attorney general of the Dutch Supreme Court. The Remmelink Commission undertook a careful nationwide study of euthanasia in the Netherlands, and the following year reported its findings. In a country of fifteen million people, there had been roughly 130,000 deaths in 1990. Extrapolating from official reports as well as interviews with doctors, the Commission estimated that 2,300 deaths, 1.8 percent of the total, had resulted from euthanasia, while another 400 could be classified as physician-assisted suicide. However, only 486 of these deaths had been reported on the death certificate as euthanasia or assisted suicide. In nearly all of the 2,700 cases, however, the guidelines established by the Rotterdam court as well as by the Medical Society had been met, with the obvious exception of reporting.

The Remmelink group did, however, uncover one disturbing feature of the Dutch practice. In an additional thousand cases, the patient had not been competent when the doctor had injected the drugs, raising questions about whether the family had been involved or the doctor had arbitrarily and solely decided on the procedure. (The Dutch do not use the term "euthanasia" for such cases, reserving it solely for instances in which the patient voluntarily requests the doctor to act.) For opponents of assisted suicide, these thousand deaths clearly pointed to physician abuse, and they direly warned of the slippery slope on which doctors would choose who would live and who would die, a Nazi-like extermination of the very old, the very young, the sick, the disabled, and those whose illnesses placed heavy financial or emotional burdens on their families.

The Dutch investigators did look closely at these thousand cases, and did not come to such a frightful conclusion. Over half of the patients had previously while competent expressed an interest in euthanasia, and most were moribund at the time of the lethal injections. This information, however, came from doctor interviews, and while one might surmise that in a majority of the instances the actions probably would have been approved by the patients if they had been able to voice their sentiments, one can also conclude that there were cases of involuntary euthanasia. Whether the incidence of such abuse is greater in the Netherlands than elsewhere is impossible to say. The vast majority of deaths in the United States are not investigated, nor are there autopsies except under suspicious circumstances. A very sick person dies, the attending physician signs a certificate attributing death to the disease, and that is the end of the matter. Anecdotal information as well as some surveys indicate that in at least some instances doctors hasten death, and without the open consent of the patient.

To supporters of physician-assisted suicide, the Remmelink findings proved reassuring. The number of euthanasia and assisted suicide deaths accounted for only a small fraction (2.1 percent) of the total deaths in the country; even if one added in the estimated one thousand nonvoluntary deaths, the total still amounted to less than 3 percent. Moreover, doctors did not practice euthanasia on all who requested it; physicians acceded to only one request in three. As far as could be determined, doctors euthanized only persons in the terminal stage of illness; 87 percent of the patients had been expected to die within a week, and another 12 percent within a month.

One of the main concerns of opponents of euthanasia, as well as the stated policy of American medical associations, is the effect that such practice will have on physicians. Giving doctors legal power to end life, they claim, subverts the entire basis of the healing arts, and will not only demean the profession but dehumanize doctors as well. For evidence they point to the Dutch Pediatric Association, which in 1992 issued guidelines on how physicians should handle the euthanasia of children and newborns. In deciding whether to end the life of a severely handicapped newborn, doctors would judge the expected quality of life for the infant, and if prospects seemed dim that the child could lead even a semblance of a normal life, then euthansia would be justified. In February 1993 the Ministry of Justice proposed expanding guidelines to allow doctors to perform "active medical intervention to cut short life without an express request." In April of the same year a court formally approved the euthanasia of psychiatric patients, after a doctor helped end the life of a woman who stated that she wanted to die after losing two of her children and going through a divorce.

In 1995 a second nationwide investigation, consisting of two major studies, followed up on the original Remmelink report, and seemed to cut the ground from under the slippery-slope argument. One study compared practices in 1995 to those in 1990, while the second sought to assess the notification procedure that had been formulated by the Ministry of Justice and the Royal Dutch Medical Society in the early 1990s and that had been enacted into law in 1994.

The first study team, led by Paul J. van der Maas, found that practices in 1995 differed little from those in 1990. Euthanasia had become somewhat more frequent, but they attributed this to the aging of the population as well as an increase in mortality from cancer, the usual underlying disease in cases of euthanasia. Physician-assisted suicide remained rare, according to van der Maas, because it is slower than euthanasia and also because the Dutch draw no moral distinction between the two. As in 1990, nearly all of the euthanasia cases involved patients suffering from terminal sickness, with only a short time left to live. The number of cases in which the patient did not explicitly request the doctor to act declined somewhat from 1990. The report concluded that the Netherlands had not started down a slippery slope and that Dutch doctors continued to practice euthanasia carefully and only under compelling circumstances.

The second study showed that the incidence of doctors reporting euthanasia or assisted suicide had risen from 18 percent in 1990 to 41 percent in 1995, indicating that a majority of the cases still went unreported. While agreeing on the need for some form of oversight, the medical profession found burdensome the multiple levels of legal review, and also resented the fact that euthanasia technically remained a crime, despite the official guidelines. For many doctors, the slightest chance of criminal prosecution, or even of investigation by the Ministry of Justice, justified attributing death to an underlying illness rather than to euthanasia.

What effect does practicing euthanasia have on Dutch doctors? Have they become Nazi-like arbiters of death for the aged and infirm, or have they expanded the role of physician to include compassionate end-of-life treatment? The relatively low incidence of euthanasia would seem to negate the first view, although the number of involuntary cases would indicate that some doctors have chosen to act on their own. However, this arrogation of power is not limited to doctors in the Netherlands. In the United States about 70 percent of hospital deaths occur after a decision has been made, sometimes by the family, sometimes by the family and the doctor, and in some cases by the doctor alone, to forgo further treatment; in the Netherlands that figure is only 20 percent. In addition, for treatment of pain both countries allow the use of morphine and other opioids in doses that could lead to death, the so-called double effect. The Dutch are just much more open about what they are doing.

Probably the one aspect about the practice that vexes most doctors is the reporting requirement and the fact that their decisions to help patients end their lives, decisions based on knowledge of the patient and of the disease, are reviewed by nonmedical bureaucrats. About three-fifths of all physician-assisted deaths go unreported, with doctors claiming that they want to spare the patients' families and themselves the scrutiny of an inquiry. Since 1981 only twenty doctors have been prosecuted for violating the guidelines, and only six have received prison sentences—all suspended. With the exception of the reporting requirement, Dutch doctors have not abused the system in any significant way.

———

In 1994 Netherlands television broadcast an actual euthanasia. The hour-long documentary tracked the last four months in the life of a former restaurateur, Cornelis van Wednel de Joode, 63, called Kees, who suffered from amyotrophic lateral sclerosis, commonly known in this country as Lou Gehrig's disease, or ALS. The other key actors in the drama were his wife, Antoinette, and his doctor, Wilfred van Oijen. The drama showed a caring physician who obviously knew Kees well and who was clearly not rushing his patient to die.

De Joode first raised the issue of euthanasia in December, but spoke of it in future terms, a decision and an act for later. By February, however, his physical condition had deteriorated rapidly; confined to a wheelchair, he could barely speak and often used an alphabet board in his lap to form messages that his wife relayed to the doctor. Part of the conversation that ensued went as follows:

> WIFE: "He doesn't want to go to hospital. And no artificial respiration either. He'd be a vegetable. . . ."
>
> DOCTOR: "You say that you want to make your own decision, meaning: I want to decide when I want to stop living."

KEES: "Yeah. . . . We mustn't wait any longer. . . ."

DOCTOR: "We should consult a second doctor so he can still talk to you as I am doing now. It may not be possible [to talk] in three weeks."

KEES: "It will be necessary to ask a second doctor to come now. We mustn't wait. . . ."

DOCTOR: "No—You are upset, Kees, aren't you? Come, here's a handkerchief. There, there. Take my handkerchief. . . ."

WIFE: "Let's change the subject. Otherwise he won't stop."

DOCTOR: "No, it's all right. Wait. It's understandable. It's the most essential decision he'll ever make. . . ."

A second doctor arrived a few days later, by which time Kees could no longer talk and relied completely on the alphabet board. The doctor went over the situation with Kees, and explained in graphic detail what would happen in the final stages of ALS, including the high possibility that he would suffocate on his own saliva. Kees agreed, and asked if he had "passed the test." The doctor agreed that he had passed.

Although now technically entitled to be euthanized, Kees kept delaying, until he finally decided that he would die on his sixty-third birthday, March 3, 1994. Dr. Oijen arrived shortly before eight in the evening, to find Kees sitting in his wheelchair and sipping a glass of port through a straw.

KEES (TO DOCTOR): "Is it rough for you too?"

DOCTOR: "Well, my feet were dragging a bit on the way here." (Both laugh nervously)

DOCTOR: "But should we wait much longer, Kees, or do you think. . . ."

WIFE: "Let him finish his port."

DOCTOR: "Of course."

KEES (TOASTING DOCTOR): "Your health."

DOCTOR: "Thank you."

WIFE (READING WHAT KEES SPELLS OUT ON THE LETTER BOARD): "Let . . . us . . . post . . . pone . . . not . . . any . . . longer. Let's go."

DOCTOR: "If you wish, Kees, we could do it tomorrow."

{ *Lethal Judgments* }

But Kees turned his wheelchair and headed into the bedroom. After his wife dressed him for bed, the doctor came in with a syringe. (Dutch doctors typically use two injections, the first a barbiturate to put the patient to sleep, and then a curare derivative to stop the heart.) Dr. Oijen explained to Kees that he would doze off, and sleep peacefully without dreams; it would take less than ten minutes for the medication to pass through his bloodstream. After giving him the first needle, Oijen sat with his arm around Antoinette, watching Kees go to sleep. He asked her if she found this distressing, and she replied no, that he seemed so peaceful now. Then she broke down and cried. "We're doing it together . . . like we always did . . . only I can't come along now. You have to go out on your own." Oijen then administered the second injection, and sat with Antoinette as Kees died.

Then came what to many people must have seemed a surreal moment. After nearly an hour of somber, and to many people uplifting and compassionate, drama, the doctor called the city coroner to notify him of the euthanasia. The official arrived shortly, and after taking down the details, informed the widow and doctor that it would now go to the public prosecutor for evaluation.

> DOCTOR: "It's strange idea really, that a nonmedical person's going to sit in judgment."
>
> CORONER: "That's the procedure. It's for the Ministry of Justice. I'll ring the public prosecutor from here, right now. . . . And then he'll take the decision on whether to clear the body for burial. . . ."

———

While many people see the Dutch way as the future for the United States, a closer analysis of the medical culture in Holland suggests that the model may not transfer easily across the ocean. The Netherlands is a small country, prosperous, technologically advanced, democratic, with a well-educated citizenry. But it is not a miniature version of the United States. It has some fifteen million people living in an area smaller than West Virginia, and 96 percent are white and native-born. While there is a rich religious diversity, the different groups coexist peacefully and enjoy a long tradition of tolerance. The Catholic and Protestant political parties are both centrist, and the Dutch Catholic Church has long been known for its independence from the more conservative pronouncements of the Vatican.

In a country in which most people are comfortably middle class, there is also an extensive state welfare system in place. Nearly everyone in the small country is covered by either government or private health insurance that pays practically all medical expenses, thus alleviating the patient's fear of becoming a financial burden upon the family. Even nursing homes are funded by the government and are available to everyone. Dr. Herbert Cohen, who is regarded by many as the archetype of the compassionate doctor practicing euthanasia, says that physician-assisted death "is not a way out of social misery. You don't have to request euthanasia because you can't get any medical attention." In the United States, where one out of six persons has no health insurance of any sort and millions more lack full coverage, hospitalization and nursing-home care can impoverish a family. The people of Holland face practically no out-of-pocket expenses at the end of life.

In the United States, there is one general practitioner (GP) for every 6.5 specialists; in the Netherlands the ratio is 1 to 1.5. Dutch GPs live in the neighborhood of their patients, their offices are in their homes, and they make house calls when their patients are too sick to come to the office. There is a close relationship between the doctors and their patients, many of whom they have treated for decades, a relationship strikingly similar to what health care used to be in the United States before it became so technological and hospital-centered.

If anything, the trusting relationship between doctor and patient is one reason that the Dutch policy works. The doctor does not come in when a patient asks for euthanasia, give an injection, and leave. Dr. Oijen visited Kees a number of times, and stayed with his wife throughout the final act. To give another example, when Andrea de Lang chose to end her life because of the pain and debilitating effects of pancreatic cancer, her doctor stayed the entire night in her apartment with her husband, three grown children, a sister, and other friends. In Holland 40 percent of all deaths take place in the home, compared to only 15 percent in the United States.

Holland has been described as a "consensus" society. Because there is some significant opposition to euthanasia, the practice remains illegal on the books. At the same time there are official guidelines for doctors and public officials to follow. Dutch ethicist Evert Van Leeuwen thinks that the consensus among the citizenry is what makes the practice work and that the type of physician-assisted suicide that would ultimately be considered in the U.S. Supreme Court would never work in Holland. Patients cannot "demand" euthanasia, but rather must work it out with their doctors as partners in the decision process. "We do not talk in terms of rights," he says. Only about a third of those who request euthanasia get it, and unlike in the United States, the other 63 percent do not go to courts.

The practice of euthanasia appears to be growing in the Netherlands. Although the percentage of deaths caused by euthanasia remained relatively constant, requests for ending life jumped nearly 40 percent between 1990 and 1995 and have been common among those infected by the AIDS virus. The majority of requests come from people between the ages of 35 and 70 who have cancer.

Some Dutch believe that their acceptance of euthanasia as a socially useful and humane practice stems from their strong belief in individual autonomy, and interviews of those choosing to end their lives indicate that it is not the pain that is the driving force behind their decision, but their desire to control their lives, to go out when they choose and in a manner they deem respectful of human dignity. The people of Holland see euthanasia as an aspect of medical care, and like other medical procedures, it needs to be entered into carefully and with the guidance of a physician.

The United States has a much different culture. It is geographically large, and its nearly 300 million people are diverse in race, creed, and ethnic origin. It is a contentious rather than a consensus society, and in recent years there has been a growth of divisive forces fighting over a large number of issues. Regrettably, the debate has often been vitriolic, with neither side willing to accept a compromise position. Perhaps the best example of this is abortion, into which have been woven all the volatile elements of the women's movement, religious and political fundamentalism, and a host of other concerns. As some commentators have argued, America is in the grips of a culture war, and physician-assisted suicide is one of the flashpoints.

The debate has been framed in terms of rights, and the phrase "right to die," which may mean different things to different groups, has nonetheless passed into the common lexicon. The Supreme Court of the United States has held that there is a constitutionally protected liberty interest that permits people to refuse life-preserving treatment. Where the Dutch approach the issue as a matter of medical practice, in the United States it comes in the raiment of politics and law.

Even before the question of physician-assisted suicide began its trek to the high court, several groups tried to bypass state legislatures and make it law through the practice of a popular referendum. The initiative, which dates back to the Progressive era at the beginning of the twentieth century, began as a democratic reform. If legislatures would not harken to the voice of the people, then the people would act directly. The initiative required a petition signed by a certain percentage of the electorate. When enough people signed the petition, then the proposal would be placed on the ballot at the next general election. If a majority of the voters approved, the measure became law.

Once the Supreme Court, in *Cruzan,* had held that the Constitution protected the right to end treatment, groups such as the Hemlock Society began agitating to make assisted suicide legal, and in November 1991 they managed to get Initiative 119 on the ballot in the State of Washington. Entitled a "death with dignity" measure, the proposal would have authorized doctors to administer lethal injections to incurably ill patients. The patient, and no one else claiming to act for her, had to make the request in writing and had to have been diagnosed by two doctors as having less than six months to live. The attending physicians could also require psychological evaluation of the patient to ensure competence. Two impartial persons, not members of the patients' family, had to witness the written request. Finally, a physician could not be forced to provide aid in dying under 119; an unwilling doctor would have to make an effort to transfer a qualified patient to another physician who would carry out the request. If 119 had passed, the state would have become the first jurisdiction in the world to legalize a form of euthanasia. The Hemlock Society and the Washington Citizens for Death with Dignity provided the major backing for 119, arguing that the proposal would provide terminally ill people with freedom of choice.

Both proponents and opponents of the initiative flooded the state with media spots. In one ad, a hospice worker charged that "Initiative 119 would let doctors kill my patients," while in another a woman who been diagnosed as having cancer seven years earlier told how glad she was to still be alive. Yes, there had been some rough moments, and if 119 had been in effect, she might have chosen death; but she was so happy to still be alive. Supporters of the measure ran equally emotional ads, with stories of people who died agonizing deaths. One woman, Vera Belt, told how her mother had died in great pain from throat cancer after doctors had refused her pleas for help in ending her life. When Ms. Belt's sister became similarly ill, she knew what awaited her, so she killed herself by putting a gun in her mouth and pulling the trigger.

The proposal split religious and medical groups. The Catholic Church strongly opposed the measure, but more than two hundred Protestant ministers from mainstream and liberal groups endorsed it. United Church of Christ minister Dale Turner, a supporter of 119, declared, "We're on the frontier of the world," and he dismissed concerns that people would too readily choose suicide if it became so easily available. Turner, 74, said, "Nobody loves life like an old man. A person has to be pretty ill and desperate to want to leave."

Many doctors bitterly fought the proposal. They had been trained to save lives, not to take them, and they saw 119 as opening the doors to a flood of abuse. When the Washington State Medical Society debated the issue, delegates voted 5 to 1 against it, but a poll of the general membership taken earlier in the year showed doctors split roughly evenly. A survey taken a few years later showed that 12 percent of Washington State physicians had been asked to assist in a patient's suicide, and 4 percent said they had been asked to perform euthanasia. The respondents indicated that they had granted a quarter of the requests, about the same percentage as given by doctors in the Netherlands.

Although early signs indicated that Initiative 119 would pass, opponents gained ground as election day approached. Critics claim that American voters are apathetic, but 119 galvanized the populace, and voters came out in large numbers. The initiative failed by a 54 to 46 percent margin. Both sides agreed that the debate had been useful and that an important public policy issue had been raised, one that would not quietly go away. "If we don't deal with the problems raised by 119, we'll be facing this issue again and again and again," said Dr. Peter McGough, an opponent of the measure. "Saying 'No' to assisted death is not enough. Now we have a responsibility to deal with the problems that brought out this concern."

Lawyers and legal scholars played little public role in the 119 campaign, but they too could not ignore the legal questions engendered by the measure. To begin with, proponents of 119 spoke not only of a right to die and death with dignity, both of which are now generally accepted notions, but also of a *right* to physician-assisted suicide! In a *New York Times*/CBS News poll taken in the spring of 1990 on the question of whether a doctor should help a terminally ill person die, 53 percent said yes, 42 percent said no, with the rest undecided. Moreover, even before the vote on Initiative 119, courts had begun to hear arguments asserting a constitutionally protected right to assisted suicide.

In January 1987, lawyers for Hector Rodas filed a petition in Mesa County District Court in Colorado, asserting that their client had a right to assisted suicide. In particular, his attorneys requested that Rodas "be confirmed as having the constitutional and privacy rights to receive medication and medicinal agents, from a consenting health care professional or institution, which will result in a comfortable and dignified demise."

At the time, Hector Rodas was dying of self-imposed starvation and dehydration, after having won a battle in the same court a week earlier to force the Hilltop Rehabilitation Hospital to withdraw his feeding tubes and allow him to remain in the hospital until he died. Rodas had not been considered terminally ill, but the 34-year-old man had been paralyzed from the neck down and did not want to live anymore. The local court had no problem with allowing disconnection of the feeding tubes on a theory of personal autonomy, even though it recognized that such an action would lead to Rodas's death. But the magistrate had great difficulty with the request for assistance, and must have breathed a sigh of relief when Rodas died before he had to rule on the question.

———

The Hemlock Society, encouraged by the large number of votes it got in Washington, decided to try again. It lost in California, again by a thin margin, but in 1994 managed to get Measure 16, a death-with-dignity act, on the Oregon ballot. The initiative provided:

> An adult who is capable, is a resident of Oregon and has been determined by the attending physician and consulting physician to be suffering from a terminal disease, and who has voluntarily expressed his or her wish to die, may make a written request for medication for the purpose of ending his or her life in a humane and dignified manner in accordance with this act.

In addition, Measure 16 provided a number of procedural safeguards to prevent abuse and ensure that only competent patients acting voluntarily could take advantage of the law. The attending physician had to determine that the patient suffered from a terminal illness; the patient had to make two separate requests for assistance in dying, and these requests had to be witnessed by persons who were not related to the patient and who would not benefit financially from the patient's death; the doctor had to ensure informed consent by telling the patient not only about the prognosis of the disease but about available options, including pain management and hospice care; there had to be a second medical opinion on the patient's condition; if either the attending or the consulting physician believed the patient suffered from depression or another psychological disorder, then they had to recommend the patient for counseling and could not give any medication to end life; the doctor had to ask the patient to notify next of kin, but it would be the patient's choice to do so. The patient could rescind the request at any time, and at the end of the mandatory fifteen-day waiting period the doctor had to again offer the patient a chance to rescind the request. Then and only then could a doctor write a prescription for the lethal dose of medication.

Despite an intense debate and spirited opposition similar to that in Washington, Measure 16 passed, albeit by a razor-thin 51 to 49 ratio. Analysts ascribe the results to two causes. First, the Washington initiative had been the first to reach a ballot, and it met a strong and combative opposition that the sponsors had been unprepared to face. More important, the Oregon measure contained more safeguards that blunted many of the charges that had been raised in Washington about how the proposal would be misused. The president of the Washington Hemlock Society, Midge Levy, said that the Oregon backers "learned from our experience in Washington. We had not anticipated the nature of the opposition, believing initially that Hospice and Estate lawyers would be supporters whereas they became bitter opponents. Washington had some 60 percent in favor a few months before the election and every reason to expect a victory, but the opposition mobilized on a national and even international scale."

Proponents of Measure 16 did indeed learn from 119; they expected opposition from certain quarters and met it far more effectively than had been the case in Washington. Oregon has long been a progressive state, and its western tradition prizes individualism. The notion of a person controlling his or her fate appealed to many Oregonians. In addition, Measure 16 advocates received a big boost when the Oregon medical profession, unlike that in Washington, decided to stay neutral in the campaign. The proponents also countered some of the opposition by building in safeguards, thus averting some of the charges that had been hurled against 119. In Washington, for example, doctors objected to the provision allowing them to administer a lethal injection; in Oregon the doctor would be able to prescribe medication, but would not be allowed or required to administer the fatal dosage. According to Levy, "the image of a doctor injecting a terminally ill patient with a lethal dose was unacceptable to many, whereas providing a prescription did not arouse the same reaction."

Having lost at the ballot box, opponents of Measure 16 went to court in an effort to block its implementation. A collection of physicians and terminally ill and potentially ill patients, as well as representatives of residential care facilities, claimed that the act violated the First and Fourteenth Amendments to the Constitution as well as statutory rights under the Americans with Disabilities Act, the Rehabilitation Act, and the Religious Freedom Restoration Act. Fifteen days before the act would have gone into effect, Chief Judge Michael R. Hogan of the U.S. District Court for Oregon agreed and struck the law down as unconstitutional since it provided insufficient safeguards to prevent an incompetent terminally ill patient from committing suicide. Upon appeal, however, the Ninth Circuit summarily reversed Hogan and ordered him to dismiss the complaint because the federal courts did not have jurisdiction.

In a final effort to block the death-with-dignity law, opponents managed to get their own initiative on the ballot in the fall of 1997. Measure 51, if it had passed, would have repealed the physician-assisted suicide law, and it had strong backing from the Catholic Church. Too strong, in the opinion of many voters, who resented what they saw as the church's efforts to impose its views on the state. "Religion is fine," said taxi driver Lou Galaxy. "Believe what you want to believe. But I liked the slogan of the committee running those ads: 'Don't shove your religion down my throat.'" Barbara Oskamp, 66, suffers from a brain tumor and fears a painful, lingering death. Measure 16 brought her "a sense of peace," and she resented religious groups trying to take it away from her. "I accept it when people of other religions tell me it is wrong for them. We all have different religious beliefs. But please, keep your religious beliefs to yourself."

Measure 51 failed by a wide margin, with six out of ten voters declaring they wanted to keep the assisted suicide law on the books, a margin larger than had voted for Measure 16 in the first place. The final hurdle to its implementation fell when Attorney General Janet Reno declared that doctors who used the law to prescribe lethal drugs to terminally ill patients would not be prosecuted. Reno claimed that a policy statement by Thomas A. Constantine, the administrator of the Drug Enforcement Agency in November 1997, had been issued without her knowledge and consent. Constantine had warned that the government would impose severe sanctions on any doctor who prescribed lethal dosages.

By the time of the second ballot, however, the issue of whether physician-assisted suicide constituted a protected right had been litigated in the federal courts and had been heard by the United States Supreme Court.

CHAPTER 6

Assisted Suicide in the Lower Courts

Even as interest groups sought to bypass legislatures through initiatives, other supporters of physician-assisted suicide went to court in efforts to overturn existing statutes criminalizing such practice. The first case to test a state's assisted suicide law in federal court arose in the state of Washington, the same state where Initiative 119 had been so vigorously debated in 1991. On January 29, 1994, three terminally ill patients, five doctors whose practice included the treatment of such patients, and a nonprofit organization called Compassion in Dying filed suit in the federal district court in Seattle. The suit challenged a Washington statute that held "a person is guilty of promoting a suicide attempt when he knowingly causes or aids another person to attempt suicide." Promoting a suicide constituted a class C felony, punishable by imprisonment for up to five years and a fine of up to ten thousand dollars. The Washington law had been on the books in one form or another since 1854, but had rarely been enforced. Even Compassion in Dying, while seemingly operating in violation of the statute, had never been threatened with prosecution. The state, it should be noted, had no law prohibiting suicide or attempted suicide.

The three patients, who all used pseudonyms, were each suffering from a terminal illness when the suit was originally filed. "Jane Roe," a 69-year-old retired pediatrician, had been almost completely bedridden and in constant pain since June 1993, as cancer had metastisized throughout her skeleton. "John Doe," a 44-year-old artist, had been diagnosed with AIDS in 1991, and his physical condition had deteriorated consistently since that time. He had also been the primary caregiver for his long-term companion, who had died of AIDS in June 1991. Both of these patients died before the case came to trial. The third patient, 69-year-old "James Poe," suffered from emphysema, which caused him a constant sensation of suffocating, and he had to take morphine on a regular basis to calm the panic reaction. All three patients were mentally competent, and all wished to commit suicide by taking physician-prescribed drugs.

The five physicians regularly treated terminally ill patients. Harold Glucksberg was an assistant professor of oncology at the University of Washington School of Medicine. In his declaration to the court, Glucksberg had written:

> Pain management at this stage often requires the patient to choose between enduring unrelenting pain or surrendering an alert mental state because the dose of drugs adequate to alleviate the pain will impair consciousness. Many patients will choose one or the other of these options; however, some patients do not want to end their days racked with pain or in a drug-induced stupor. For some patients pain cannot be managed even with aggressive use of drugs.

The other doctors included John P. Geyman, chair of the Department of Family Medicine at the University of Washington School of Medicine; Thomas A. Preston, chief of cardiology at the Pacific Medical Center in Seattle; Abigail Halperin, a family practitioner who occasionally treated patients with terminal illnesses; and Peter Shalit, an internist whose practice included a large number of patients with HIV or AIDS. Dr. Halperin and Dr. Shalit also held clinical instructorships at the University of Washington School of Medicine.

Compassion in Dying, a nonprofit organization, provided information, counseling, and assistance to terminally ill patients considering suicide and to their families. The organization had a strict protocol regarding the eligibility of people it would help. Patients had to be terminally ill and, in the judgment of the primary care physician, mentally competent and able to understand the consequences of their decisions. Requests had to come from the patient, in writing or on videotape, at least three times, with an interval of forty-eight hours between the second and third request. The organization would not assist anyone who expressed ambivalence or uncertainty about committing suicide, and if members of the immediate family raised objections, Compassion in Dying would not help.

The plaintiffs all challenged the Washington law, but on somewhat differing grounds. The patients alleged that they had a constitutionally protected liberty interest under the Fourteenth Amendment's Due Process Clause to secure physician assistance for suicide without undue governmental interference. They also attacked the statute on equal protection grounds. The physicians claimed that the Fourteenth Amendment protected their right to practice medicine consistent with their best professional judgment, including the right to assist competent terminally ill patients end their lives. Compassion in Dying feared that in carrying out its mission of assisting terminally ill patients in committing suicide, it could be criminally prosecuted for its activities "in assisting dying persons as they exercise their alleged constitutional right to hasten their own deaths."

Chief Judge Barbara Rothstein began her legal analysis, handed down on May 3, 1994, by granting the plaintiffs' claim of a liberty interest. The Supreme Court, she noted, had established "through a long line of cases that personal decisions relating to marriage, procreation, contraception, family relationships, child rearing and education are constitutionally protected." She cited the Court's decision in *Planned Parenthood v. Casey* (1992) that matters "involving the most intimate and personal choices a person may make in a lifetime, choices central to personal dignity and autonomy, are central to the liberty protected by the Fourteenth Amendment." Although *Casey* dealt with abortion, Rothstein found the decision of a terminally ill person to end his or her own life to be of the same category of "the most intimate and personal choices" and "central to personal dignity and autonomy."

Similarly, the Supreme Court in *Casey* had spoken of the suffering of the pregnant woman, which "is too intimate and personal for the State to insist, without more, upon its own vision of the woman's role, however dominant that vision has been in the course of our history and our culture." The district court therefore concluded "that the suffering of a terminally ill person cannot be deemed any less intimate or personal, or any less deserving of protection from unwarranted governmental interference, than that of a pregnant woman."

The court also found a liberty interest under the *Cruzan* decision, in which Chief Justice Rehnquist had held "that the United States Constitution would grant a competent person a constitutionally protected right to refuse lifesaving hydration and nutrition." The court then asked whether a constitutional difference could be drawn between "refusal or withdrawal of medical treatment which results in death, and the situation in this case involving competent, terminally ill individuals who wish to hasten death by self-administering drugs prescribed by a physician." "From a constitutional perspective," Rothstein concluded, "the court does not believe that a distinction can be drawn between refusing life-sustaining medical treatment and physician-assisted suicide by an uncoerced, mentally competent, terminally ill adult."

But as both *Cruzan* and *Casey* showed, liberty interests are not absolute, and the question then became what standard of review to use in determining if the state had trespassed onto constitutionally protected territory. The Court adopted the standard enunciated in *Casey,* whether the "state regulation imposes an undue burden on a woman's ability to make [a] decision" concerning whether or not to procure an abortion. Applying that analysis, the court then looked at the two interests the state had put forward in justification of the statute, preventing suicide and preventing undue influence and abuse.

The state had a very weak case to begin with, since Washington did not prohibit either suicide or attempted suicide, and in 1975 had repealed a previous law that did in fact bar attempted suicide. While conceding that the state had a strong interest in deterring suicide by young people, the court drew a sharp distinction between abruptly cutting a young life short and the situation of terminally ill patients, for whom preventing suicide meant only the prolongation of an often painful dying process. While the state had a legitimate interest in protecting the young, it had gone too far in extending the prohibition to terminally ill patients.

The state's second interest, protecting people from undue influence and abuse, has been one of the major arguments utilized by opponents of assisted suicide, who fear that when a person becomes elderly and a burden on the family, the person will be subject to pressure to "take the easy way out" for the sake of the family. But here the court found little to distinguish between permitting a withdrawal of medical treatment that leads to death and providing drugs that lead to the same desired result. As for the potential risks and abuses, tests already existed to evaluate the mental competency of the patient as well as the voluntariness of the decision. "Undoubtedly the legislature can devise regulations which would set up a mechanism for ensuring that people who decide to commit physician-assisted suicide are not acting pursuant to abuse, coercion or undue influence from third parties."

Having found that the state did impose an undue burden on the exercise of a liberty interest protected by the Fourteenth Amendment, Judge Rothstein then turned to the most interesting part of her analysis, equal protection. The Fourteenth Amendment's Equal Protection Clause, she noted, "is essentially a direction that all persons similarly situated should be treated alike." In equal protection analysis, a higher standard of review, that of strict scrutiny, is used, as opposed to the undue-burden standard of a liberty interest. The plaintiffs had claimed that Washington State law unconstitutionally distinguished between two groups of similarly situated people, those on life support or under medical treatment whose withdrawal would mean death and those who were likewise terminally ill, but not on life-sustaining equipment or treatment. The Washington Natural Death Act clearly stated that "adult persons have the fundamental right to control the decisions relating to the rendering of their own health care, including the decision to have the life sustaining treatment withheld or withdrawn, in instances of a terminal condition or permanent unconscious condition."

The court agreed, finding that no significant difference existed between adult, mentally competent, terminally ill patients on life support, who could decide to end their suffering by turning off the equipment, and adult, mentally competent, terminally ill patients who wished to end their suffering by committing suicide. By making such a distinction, Washington "creates a situation in which the fundamental rights of one group are burdened while those of a similarly situated group are not." The state's law, therefore, also violated the Fourteenth Amendment's Equal Protection Clause.

Both sides had asked for summary judgment, but Judge Rothstein declined to give to all the plaintiffs what they had asked. She granted summary judgment in favor of the plaintiff patients, and for the doctors insofar as they "purport to raise claims on behalf of their terminally ill patients." But she denied judgment insofar as they raised any claims on their own behalf. Similarly, she denied judgment for Compassion in Dying, since it also sought relief for itself as opposed to its clients. Finally, Judge Rothstein declined to enter an injunction barring the state from enforcing the law, on the grounds that the responsibility for enforcing criminal laws rests primarily on county prosecuting attorneys, and not on the attorney general, who had been named as a defendant.

Proponents of assisted suicide hailed Judge Rothstein's decision. Ralph Mero, a Unitarian minister who served as executive director of Compassion in Dying, said he expected a "tremendous increase" in the number of people coming to the organization for aid. "Today, every time I pick up the phone, there are three more people on voice mail asking for help." Just as predictably, opponents attacked the ruling. The Roman Catholic bishops of Washington, who had played a leading role in fighting Initiative 119, declared that assisted suicide "undermines the moral integrity of the medical profession whose duty it is to heal and comfort, not kill. And it tramples on our conviction that life, no matter how feeble or impaired, is a sacred gift from God."

William F. Buckley, in his nationally syndicated column, attacked Rothstein's decision as one more unreasonable expansion of the so-called right of privacy, and said he saw no difference between a doctor who prescribed lethal medication and a mechanic "who plants a bomb under your car, runs an electrical line to your window sill but leaves it to you to depress the button when your wife enters the car." Once again, he charged, judges had usurped the right of the people to decide such matters through their elected representatives.

The State of Washington appealed Judge Rothstein's decision, and a panel of the Court of Appeals for the Ninth Circuit, consisting of Eugene A. Wright, John T. Noonan Jr., and Diarmuid F. O'Scannlain, heard arguments on December 7, 1994. By a vote of 2 to 1, the panel reversed the district court. In an opinion written by Judge Noonan, the majority held that the district court's conclusion that the Washington statute deprived plaintiffs of both a liberty interest protected by the Fourteenth Amendment and equal protection could not be sustained.

Noonan noted that the lower court had relied on the wording in *Casey* to analogize between the privacy involved in pregnancy and similar intimacy in dying. In a remarkably refreshing comment, he declared that "any reader of judicial opinions knows they often attempt a generality of expression and a sententiousness of phrase that extend far beyond the problem addressed. It is commonly accounted an error to lift sentences or even paragraphs out of context and insert the abstracted thought into a wholly different context." Noonan found the district court's effort to equate the terms "personal dignity and autonomy" as used in *Casey* with the decision to choose death completely inapposite.

The category created is inherently unstable. The depressed twenty-one year old, the romantically-devastated twenty-eight year old, the alcoholic forty-year old who choose suicide are also expressing their views of the existence, meaning, the universe, and life; they are also asserting their personal liberty. . . . The attempt to restrict such rights to the terminally ill is illusory. If such liberty exists in this context, as *Casey* asserted in the context of reproductive rights, every man and woman in the United States must enjoy it. . . . This conclusion is a *reductio ad absurdum.*

Noonan's phrasing of the argument, for which he relied heavily on an article by a longtime opponent of assisted suicide, Professor Yale Kamisar of Michigan, is indeed an absurdity in the form stated, but in so stating it he avoided coming to grips with the heart of the autonomy argument. If people are truly autonomous, and if that autonomy is protected by the law (either as a Fourteenth Amendment liberty interest or as a Ninth Amendment reserved right), then suicide is an option that must be open to one who is adult and competent. The three examples Noonan cited are all, arguably, not competent, and there certainly is a significant difference between the alcoholic of whatever age and a terminally ill patient in great pain, also of whatever age.

Noonan went on to attack Judge Rothstein's ruling on other grounds. While *Cruzan* certainly dealt with end-of-life issues, the Supreme Court had made it quite clear that the right to die it enunciated was circumscribed by a state's interest in preserving life, a portion of *Cruzan* ignored in the lower court ruling. He dismissed the lower court's analysis as lacking "foundation in the traditions of our nation" and noted that "in the two hundred and five years of our existence no constitutional right to aid in killing oneself has ever been asserted and upheld by a court of final jurisdiction." Noonan went on to lecture Rothstein on the importance of judicial restraint. "Unless the federal judiciary is to be a floating constitutional convention, a federal court should not invent a constitutional right unknown to the past and antithetical to the defense of human life that has been a chief responsibility of our constitutional government." Noonan also found that the facial invalidation of the statute was unwarranted by the *Casey* precedent and, most important, that the district court had completely ignored the State of Washington's real interest in protecting life. In addition, the lower court had entered a judgment on behalf of two plaintiffs already dead.

"This unheard-of judgment was a nullity." Finally, Noonan dismissed the equal rights analysis by stating that ending life support for a terminally ill patient and letting the underlying condition bring on death was a far different thing from actively terminating life.

The strongest part of Noonan's argument lay in his analysis of the state's interest, although unlike in *Cruzan,* where Rehnquist had made it clear that a right to die existed although circumscribed by state interests, Noonan completely ignored the end-of-life issues for those in pain from an incurable disease. In part, Noonan wanted to rectify what he saw as a major error in Judge Rothstein's analysis, her dismissal of alleged state interests.

Noonan listed five such interests: (1) the interest in not having doctors act as the killers of their patients; (2) the interest in not subjecting the elderly and the infirm to psychological pressure to consent to their own deaths; (3) the interest in protecting the poor and minorities, who would be especially susceptible, from exploitation; (4) the interest in protecting all of the handicapped from societal indifference and antipathy; and (5) the interest in preventing abuses similar to those in the Netherlands. In his opinion, Noonan made no reference to Judge Rothstein's extended analysis of which standard of review to utilize, but in dismissing both the liberty interest and equal protection arguments, he adopted what amounted to a simple rational-basis test. The state had legitimate interests, and therefore the statute was constitutional.

Noonan was undoubtedly right in his assertion that the state has interests in preserving life, but if the lower court decision went too far in its efforts to address the concerns of the terminally ill, the majority opinion in the court of appeals had little to say on that score, except a sort of apologia at the end. Noonan agreed that compassion is a great virtue and that "no one can read the accounts of the sufferings of the deceased plaintiffs supplied by their declarations, or the accounts of the sufferings of their patients supplied by the physicians, without being moved by them." But "compassion cannot be the compass of a federal judge. That compass is the Constitution of the United States.

Where, as here in the case of Washington, the statute of a state comports with that compass, the validity of the statute must be upheld."

Judge Eugene A. Wright entered a relatively brief dissent, in which he asserted that the real right involved was that of privacy, and the "right to die with dignity falls squarely within the privacy right recognized by the Supreme Court." Wright agreed with the lower court that no constitutional distinction could be drawn between refusing life-sustaining treatment and taking a physician-prescribed drug to hasten death, and he pointed to a higher authority for this argument—Justice Scalia's concurrence in *Cruzan,* in which he had said that "starving oneself to death is no different from putting a gun to one's temple as far as the common-law definition of suicide is concerned."

In answer to Judge Noonan's appeal for judicial restraint, Wright argued that substantive due process has always evolved to meet new societal needs. An appeal to history and tradition is useless where medicine is concerned because of the rapid changes taking place in that field. In essence, one has to craft a law dealing with the medical realities of the late twentieth century, not that of the late eighteenth. But even if we appeal to history and tradition, Wright found the values of self-determination and privacy regarding personal decisions to have always been highly prized. "No right is held more sacred, or more carefully guarded, by the common law, than the right of every individual to the possession and control of his own person, free from all restraint or interference of others unless by clear and unquestioned authority. The right to die with dignity accords with the American values of self-determination and privacy regarding personal decisions."

––––––

Losing parties in the courts of appeal often ask for a rehearing *en banc,* that is, by the full circuit court rather than by a three-judge panel, although such requests are rarely granted. But in this case, the Ninth Circuit agreed on August 1, 1995, and heard oral argument before a panel of eleven judges on October 26,

1995. By a vote of 8 to 3, the court reversed Noonan's decision and found that the Washington State statute violated the Due Process Clause of the Fourteenth Amendment.

Judge Stephen Reinhardt, in a lengthy forty-six-page opinion for the majority, described as "extremely thoughtful" Judge Rothstein's lower court opinion. Noonan had gone out of his way to declare the lower court decision in favor of two dead plaintiffs absurd. Reinhardt drew the obvious parallel to the Supreme Court's initial decision in *Roe v. Wade,* where the original plaintiff was no longer pregnant but the Court recognized that other women would become pregnant. A case is not mooted when the controversy is capable of repetition, yet evading review. The fact that two of the original plaintiffs had died before the case came to trial did not matter; the issue they raised remained important, because other people would also suffer end-of-life crises, and they, too, might die before their cases could come to trial.

The important thing about the Ninth Circuit's opinion is that Judge Reinhardt decided to focus his opinion entirely on the Due Process Clause and therefore did not feel it necessary to deal with the equal protection analysis. Although he fleshed out his argument with copious references, Reinhardt made it clear from the start that he believed the Constitution protected a right to die, and he then phrased the question as whether "prohibiting physicians from prescribing life-ending medication for use by terminally ill patients who wish to die violates the patients' due process rights." While recognizing that, as in all liberty interests, a balancing was required between the rights of the individual and the legitimate interests of the state, the larger panel, unlike Judge Noonan, would impose more than the simple rational-basis test.

The court quickly found that a liberty interest existed, and like Judge Rothstein, the panel found "compelling similarities between right-to-die cases and abortion cases." The majority went further than the district court, however, in noting that the balancing test might yield different outcomes at different points along the life cycle. In *Roe,* the Court had utilized a trimester arrangement, in which the woman's interests and choices were paramount in the first trimester, while the state's interests took precedence in the last trimester. So in determining end-of-life decisions, differing circumstances could dictate differing outcomes—a conclusion that was a direct repudiation of Judge Noonan's *reductio ad absurdum.*

The key to the panel's analysis is that Judge Reinhardt at all times focused on what he considered the larger liberty interest, namely, the right to die, which had already been articulated by the Supreme Court in *Cruzan.* Judge Noonan, by defining the alleged liberty interest only as a right to assisted death, could ignore the larger issue, and in doing so could dismiss much of the district court's analysis. Reinhardt's approach was more encompassing. "We do not ask simply whether there is a liberty interest in receiving 'aid in killing oneself' because such a narrow interest could not exist in the absence of a broader and more important underlying interest—the right to die. In short, it is the end and not the means that defines the liberty interest."

Once the court framed the argument in these terms, with a majority believing that the "larger" issue constituted the right to die, then it could formulate the liberty interest, identify an appropriate standard of review, and hold Washington's prohibition on assisting suicide against that standard. But the Ninth Circuit actually went further in its expansive reading of what substantive due process means. It began with Justice John Marshall Harlan's dissent in *Poe v. Ullman* (1961), in which he argued that "the full scope of the liberty guaranteed by the Due Process Clause is a rational continuum which, broadly speaking, includes a freedom from all substantial arbitrary impositions and purposeless restraints." Harlan had hinted in his dissent that some liberty interests are weightier than others, and according to Reinhardt, the Supreme Court in recent cases, including *Cruzan,* appeared "heading towards the formal adoption of the continuum approach, along with a balancing test, in substantive due process cases generally." But the problem then became what criteria courts would use in determining the scope of the continuum and the values it placed along it.

Again responding to Noonan's decision, Reinhardt indicated that history and tradition could play only a limited role in such judgments. Times changed, and "were history our sole guide, the Virginia anti-miscegenation statute that the Court overturned in *Loving v. Virginia* (1967), as violative of substantive due process and the Equal Protection Clause, would still be in force because such anti-miscegenation laws were commonplace both when the United States was founded and when the Fourteenth Amendment was adopted." Moreover, or so Reinhardt claimed, the Supreme Court itself had "rejected the view that substantive due process protects rights or liberties only if they possess a historical pedigree."

Reinhardt then went into an analysis of historical attitudes toward suicide and of changes that had taken place, citing polls that showed that a large majority of Americans endorsed recent legal decisions that granted terminally ill patients the right to terminate treatment, discussing a variety of books and articles, and giving examples of people who had taken their own life.

The analysis of the liberty interest under both *Casey* and *Cruzan* followed in general the outline of the lower court, but with the difference that after finding the liberty interest, Reinhardt did not dismiss the state's concerns as easily as Judge Rothstein had done. Reinhardt identified six important state interests: (1) a general interest, preserving life; (2) a more specific interest, preventing suicide; (3) avoiding involvement of third parties in the decision and precluding arbitrary, unfair, or undue influence; (4) protecting family members and loved ones; (5) protecting the integrity of the medical profession; and (6) avoiding adverse consequences that might ensue if the statute were found unconstitutional.

The difference in wording from Noonan's list is instructive. Noonan apparently started with an assumption that if a right to die existed, under *Cruzan* it was limited and had to take a secondary role to the state's interests. His balancing is not a balancing at all, but a simple rational-basis test. Reinhardt starts with the assumption that the right to die is an important liberty interest, fully protected by substantive due process, and that while there is a continuum, the individual's rights are presumed to trump those of the state, absent some compelling reason. In his analysis of the six state interests, as balanced against those of the individual, Reinhardt found no such reason. Reinhardt did not say that the state could not regulate physician-assisted suicide or that it might not establish procedures to limit that choice to a particular group of people, but he found the total ban as embodied in the state statute went too far. "By adopting appropriate, reasonable, and properly drawn safeguards, Washington could ensure that people who choose to have their doctors prescribe lethal doses of medication are truly competent and meet all requisite standards."

Reinhardt also chose to answer one final point in Noonan's opinion, the call for judicial restraint, so that courts should not be involved in this sort of policy making. Reinhardt agreed that matters involving life and death should not be made by courts. He then stood the argument on its head by declaring that "by permitting the *individual* to exercise the right to *choose* we are following the constitutional mandate to take such decisions out of the hands of the government, both state and federal, and to put them where they rightly belong, in the hands of the people. We are allowing people to make the decisions that so profoundly affect their very existence—and precluding the state from intruding excessively into that critical realm." The decision did not force anyone to commit suicide. "Those who believe strongly that death must come without physician assistance are free to follow that creed, be they doctors or patients. They are not free, however, to force their views, their religious convictions, or their philosophies on all the other members of a democratic society, and to compel those whose values differ with theirs to die painful, protracted and agonizing deaths."

There were three dissents from the majority opinion. Judge Robert R. Beezer believed that terminally ill patients did not have a fundamental right to physician-assisted suicide, a right he could find neither "deeply rooted in this Nation's history and tradition" nor implicit in the concept of ordered liberty. His dissent rejected the majority notion that *Casey* supported the creation of a right to assisted suicide in any manner, and he argued that in any case, abortion rights were no longer fundamental after *Casey*, and thus were inapplicable to termination of a viable life. Since the asserted liberty interest was not fundamental, a rational-basis standard would be acceptable, although Beezer believed that the law would survive strict scrutiny as well. Similarly, he thought the equal protection argument could also be measured on a rational basis, because the plaintiffs' challenge did not involve either a fundamental right or a suspect classification. Judges Ferdinand F. Fernandez and Andrew J. Kleinfeld joined Beezer's dissent, but each added a reservation. Fernandez said that nothing in either the majority or the minority opinion convinced him of the existence of any constitutional right to suicide and that end-of-life choices ought to be left to the legislature and not the courts to decide. Kleinfeld also doubted that there was any constitutional right to suicide, and he could see a clear difference between withdrawing from treatment and actively overdosing on lethal drugs.

———

On the East Coast, Dr. Timothy Quill, the doctor who had leaped into national prominence with his admission that he had helped one of his patients commit suicide, launched a legal attack against the law under which local prosecutors had tried to indict him. In July 1994 Quill, along with two other doctors, Samuel C. Klagsbrun and Howard A. Grossman, brought suit in the Southern District of New York to have New York's ban on assisted suicide declared unconstitutional. Three terminally ill patients had originally joined the suit, but all of them had died before the case went to trial, leaving only the physicians.

In his declaration, Quill explained that due to the criminal investigation following the death of his patient, he had been afraid to provide other terminally ill patients with barbiturates for fear of violating the criminal law, a complaint made by the other two doctors as well. They sought an injunction to bar enforcement of those portions of the New York Penal Code that made assisting suicide a second-degree felony (manslaughter).

The state asserted that no actual case or controversy existed, and therefore the suit should be dismissed as nonjusticiable. Although Chief Judge Thomas P. Griesa held that the action did in fact provide a justiciable controversy, he went on to rule that patients did not have any fundamental right to physician-assisted suicide and that the state laws criminalizing assisted suicide did not violate the Equal Protection Clause.

The first issue, that of justiciability, might not have arisen had any of the original patient plaintiffs lived long enough, but unlike Judge Rothstein, Griesa did not keep them listed as plaintiffs, nor did he invoke the "capable of repetition, yet evading review" rationale used in the Ninth Circuit. The state had argued that the doctors had no standing because they could show no more than a speculative possibility of prosecution. None of them had ever been arrested, indicted, or prosecuted under the law. Griesa found this an easy question, since the Supreme Court in a number of cases had held that when challenging the constitutionality of a criminal statute, the plaintiff need not expose himself to actual prosecution.

On the second question, Griesa agreed that under the Fourteenth Amendment "there are certain subjects that are so fundamental to personal liberty that governmental invasion is either entirely prohibited or sharply limited." Like the judges in the Ninth Circuit, he too found a supporting statement in *Casey* about due process protecting "the most intimate and personal choices a person may make in a lifetime." But Griesa remained unwilling to draw the analogy between the "intimate and personal choices" relating to abortion and those made at the end of life. He found the Supreme Court's ruling in *Cruzan* less than enlightening, and as he read that decision, he concluded that "the Court stopped short of actually deciding that there is a constitutional right to terminate medical treatment necessary to sustain life, although the Court *assumed* the existence of such a right for the purpose of going on to the other issues in the case."

Since the plaintiffs read *Roe, Casey,* and *Cruzan* as embodying a due process protection of all intimate and personal choices, they believed that it should cover whether a person wanted to end her or his own life, certainly one of the most intimate and personal of all choices. According to the court, "plaintiffs' reading of these cases is too broad." One could not find any historic recognition of a right to physician-assisted suicide, even in the case of terminally ill patients. Suicide had long been considered a crime in its own right, and a majority of states imposed penalties on those who aided others to kill themselves. Even the Model Penal Code, which supposedly embodied the most enlightened thought, made it a crime to assist a suicide. As far as the court was concerned, even the very limited form of assisted suicide advocated by the plaintiffs, helping terminally ill people end their suffering, could hardly be characterized as a liberty interest protected under the Fourteenth Amendment.

The three doctors had also put forward an equal protection argument, namely, that people who wanted to end their suffering through active euthanasia were not treated equally with those already on life-sustaining treatment, whom the law allowed to terminate that treatment. Judge Griesa made short shrift of that argument as well. Did the distinction drawn by the legislature between the two classes have a reasonable and rational basis? He admitted that some people would see little or no difference, while others would see a great difference. "In any event, it is hardly unreasonable or irrational for the State to recognize a difference between allowing nature to take its course, even in the most severe situations, and intentionally using an artificial death-producing device." The state had obvious interests in preserving life and protecting vulnerable persons, and under the Constitution, in the absence of an identifiable individual right, the state had the discretion over what way it chose to protect its interests. Griesa then granted the state summary judgment in its favor.

The New York decision came down seven months after Judge Rothstein had decided the Washington decision and only a week after the latter case had been argued before the three-judge panel of the Ninth Circuit. Yet the New York case did not draw as much attention as the Washington case, and the decision mentioned no *amici* briefs filed on either side. This situation had changed dramatically when the Second Circuit heard argument on the case at the beginning of September 1995, and a significant number of groups, many of whom had also filed in the Ninth Circuit, now joined the fray on the East Coast. The case came before a panel of Roger J. Miner, Guido Calabresi, and Milton Pollack, a senior district judge from the Southern District of New York sitting by designation. Miner wrote the unanimous opinion.

One could immediately sense where Miner intended to go by his statement of the background. Where Judge Griesa had merely mentioned that the three patient-plaintiffs had died before the trial had begun, Miner quoted extensively from their declarations, in which they detailed their illness and the pain and suffering they endured. He also entered sections of the physicians' declarations and accounts of the problems they confronted in treating terminally ill patients.

Like the lower court, the Second Circuit rejected the state's claim that no justiciable issue existed. Miner not only referred to *Babbitt* and *Doe v. Bolton,* but took judicial notice that an attempt had been made to indict Dr. Quill after he acknowledged helping a patient end her life. Although New York County district attorney Robert M. Morganthau (also a named defendant) had claimed that the plaintiffs had not shown that they stood in any jeopardy, Minor quoted from a newspaper clipping reporting that Morgenthau had announced a grand jury indictment of George Delury on manslaughter charges for helping his wife commit suicide the previous summer. "The physician plaintiffs," Miner concluded, "have good reason to fear prosecution in New York County."

The court then began its inquiry into whether assisted suicide could qualify as a fundamental liberty interest. "Rights that have no textual support in the language of the Constitution but qualify for heightened judicial protection include fundamental liberties so 'implicit in the concept of ordered liberty' that 'neither liberty nor justice would exist if they were sacrificed.'" While the Supreme Court had counted privacy as among the rights protected by due process, it had been reluctant to expand the meaning of privacy and had given lower courts tenuous guidelines on how they could proceed. That line, "albeit a shaky one," could be found in *Bowers v. Hardwick* (1986), where the high court had found no fundamental right to engage in consensual sodomy, since the statutes proscribing such conduct had "ancient roots." Taking its cue from that case, the appellate court declined to define physician-assisted suicide as a right implicit in the concept of ordered liberty. And as in *Bowers,* no historical justification existed to make it so. "Indeed, the very opposite is true. The Common Law of England, as received by the American colonies, prohibited suicide and attempted suicide.... Clearly, no 'right' to assisted suicide has ever been recognized in the United States." If the Supreme Court was hesitant to expand due process rights, "then our position in the judicial hierarchy constrains us to be even more reluctant than the Court to undertake an expansive approach in this uncharted area."

Such restraint, however, seemed to evaporate as the court turned to the plaintiffs' other argument, that a denial of physician-assisted suicide violated the Equal Protection Clause. Seeking an appropriate level of review, the court reviewed those types of legislation that called for rational basis (matters of social welfare and economics), intermediate scrutiny (matters of gender and illegitimacy), and strict scrutiny (matters involving suspect classes). It then concluded that the prohibition against physician-assisted suicide fell into the class of social welfare and could be examined under a rational-basis test.

One might speculate that the appellate court took this route to avoid the perception that it was creating a new right or expanding an existing one. By treating the statute as a form of social welfare regulation, it could apply the lowest form of review and find that it made no rational sense to distinguish between allowing people to terminate treatment to hasten death and allowing people to hasten death by other means. The New

York legislature had specifically amended its laws in 1987 to allow people to refuse treatment and to direct doctors and hospitals not to resuscitate should those patients go into cardiac arrest. Three years later the state had provided for health care proxies, empowering such proxies to terminate treatment for comatose patients.

After reviewing the Supreme Court's holding in *Cruzan*, Judge Miner concluded that "it seems clear that New York does not treat similarly circumstanced people alike: those in the final stages of terminal illness who are on life-support systems are allowed to hasten their deaths by directing the removal of such systems, but those who are similarly situated, except for the previous attachment of life-sustaining equipment, are not allowed to hasten death by self-administering prescribed drugs." The court could see little difference between assisted suicide and the withholding or withdrawal of treatment.

Having found unequal treatment, the court then had to determine whether a rational basis existed for establishing such inequality. At oral argument, the state had argued that its "principal interest is in preserving the life of all its citizens at all times and under all conditions," to which Miner responded:

> But what interest can the state possibly have in requiring the prolongation of a life that is all but ended? Surely, the state's interest lessens as the potential for life diminishes. And what business is it of the state to require the continuation of agony when the result is imminent and inevitable? What concern prompts the state to interfere with a mentally competent patient's "right to define [his] own concept of existence, of meaning, of the universe, and of the mystery of human life," when the patient seeks to have drugs prescribed to end life during the final stages of a terminal illness? The greatly reduced interest of the state in preserving life compels the answer to these questions: "None."

In conclusion, the court found that New York statutes criminalizing assisted suicide violated the Equal Protection Clause, insofar as preventing a doctor from prescribing drugs to a mentally competent patient bore no rational relationship to any legitimate state interest.

Judge Guido Calabresi concurred in the judgment—that the laws as written should be struck down—but he entered a separate opinion, believing it premature to reach either the due process or equal protection analysis regarding the larger question of whether all laws prohibiting assisted suicide might fail. Calabresi began with a lengthy analysis of English and New York laws on suicide and assisted suicide, and concluded that "the bases of these statutes have been deeply eroded over the last hundred and fifty years, and few of their foundations remain in place today." As he read the history, the original reason for the statutes had been to criminalize other conduct that at the time had itself been prohibited, suicide and attempted suicide. Since then at least one form of suicide, the withdrawal of life-sustaining treatment, had become legally recognizable, and one could find little distinction between that conduct and the taking of prescribed drugs to end life. The legislature, faced by these changing conditions, had not acted affirmatively to reassert the state's policy while at the same time the older laws were unenforced.

Normally this would not make much difference, since "we regularly uphold laws whose original reason has vanished, whose fit with the rest of the legal system is dubious, whose enforcement is virtually nil, and whose continued presence on the books seems as much due to the strong inertia that the framers of our constitutions gave to the *status quo* as to any current majoritarian support." But when fundamental substantive rights are in danger, there is also "a long tradition of constitutional holdings that inertia will not do." The answer, he believed, lay in notifying legislatures of the potential unconstitutionality of a particular statute, and the legislatures should then have the opportunity either to reaffirm the law and then face the constitutional test, abandon the law, or amend the law to cure it of perceived defects. Notification could be done in a variety of ways. One was to nullify the law, as had been done here, but he would add an invitation to the legislature to reconsider the matter. This approach, he believed, not only provided a better way of courts' handling matters of such far-reaching import, but also had precedents in the Supreme Court. There the justices on a number of occasions had struck down particular laws or administrative regulations but had invited the Congress or an agency to rethink and revise the rule. Calabresi considered this law of nineteenth-century origins to be of doubtful validity and joined the majority in striking it down. But he did so in what he described as "a constitutional remand" and noted specifically that he had not dealt with the merits of the plaintiffs' case; that, he urged, should wait until the New York legislature had acted.

———

While advocates for particular interest groups, such as the Hemlock Society and the American Civil Liberties Union, cheered the decisions in the Second and Ninth Circuits, legal commentators proved considerably more hostile. Susan R. Martyn and Henry J. Bourguignon attacked what they considered the "lethal flaws" in the Second and Ninth Circuit opinions. The two opinions "mark a decisive turning point in American law that must not pass unnoticed or unchallenged." They considered the line drawn by the courts between withdrawal of treatment and active euthanasia untenable, and they wrote that "the sole purpose of this Essay is to drive home the many compelling reasons to maintain the traditional line between killing and letting die." As for the pain and suffering of terminally ill patients with unrelievable pain who voluntarily sought a doctor's help to end their lives, "we must continue to treat these rare cases, however, as tragic, isolated occurrences." Above all, the slippery slope running perilously near the surface in the two decisions had to be avoided, lest Americans repeat the same horrible pattern of events that led to euthanasia in the Netherlands.

An article in the *Harvard Civil Rights–Civil Liberties Law Review* took a different tack, that the courts had erred in limiting the right to the terminally ill. If a liberty interest existed, then bans on doctor-assisted suicide ought to be unconstitutional as applied not only to terminally ill patients but to others as well. "The case for the balance tipping in favor of the individual is clearest with respect to those who are incurably in pain or have an ailment that portends imminent death." Here the individual liberty interest clearly trumped any state interests in protecting life and regulating the medical profession.

But what about non–terminally ill individuals? If a liberty interest existed that allowed one category of people to end their lives, why should it be restricted to just that class? The authors believed an equal protection analysis would support their argument that the right had to be broader. If a non–terminally ill person suffered from terrible pain that could not be medically alleviated, why should she have to suffer with no hope of release except a death that might be years away? The notion that people who have years to live face many options for a fruitful life is not convincing to a bedridden man who cannot even get up to walk to the bathroom. There could be little difference between allowing a person who might have years to live if she stayed on dialysis to stop that treatment and die and allowing a person not on such a regimen who suffered from a debilitating, painful, but not fatal disease to end his life.

The state could adopt selective restrictions in which state interests might be considered greater than those of the individual, and this would be especially true in cases of minors and other legal incompetents, in cases where it was necessary to prevent undue influence, and in cases where the would-be suicide had minor dependents. The state could also authorize who might assist in suicides, perhaps limiting it to just physicians, and then ensure that the choice had been informed and made freely.

Perhaps the most sustained and reasoned attack on the decisions came from Chicago Law School professor Cass R. Sunstein, who argued that the Supreme Court should not invalidate state laws prohibiting physician-assisted suicide. Sunstein's argument had less to do with the morality of the issue than with the institutional dynamics of a democracy attempting to deal with a difficult problem. Even if a case could be made that there was a liberty interest and that physician-assisted suicide qualified as fundamental under the Due Process Clause, the bans could still be upheld on the grounds of the state's paramount interests. "The Court should reach this conclusion partly because of appropriate judicial modesty in the face of difficult underlying questions of value and fact; it should emphasize these institutional concerns in explaining its conclusion." Sunstein urged the high court not to short-circuit the democratic process. The question of physician-assisted suicide was not languishing due to popular indifference; to the contrary, intense discussion could be found everywhere, and in three states the issue had been put to a popular referendum. Moreover, many cases involving so-called fundamental rights, including the cases on privacy and equal protection, "are best seen not as flat declarations that the state interest was inadequate to justify the state's intrusion, but more narrowly as democracy-forcing outcomes designed to overcome problems of discrimination and desuetude." That situation did not exist here.

Practically no law review articles praised the circuit court decisions. Everyone expected the issue to go up to the Supreme Court, and given the reluctance of the Rehnquist Court to expand rights under either due process or equal protection, hardly anyone expected the appeals courts' decisions to survive. Moreover, even if one agreed with the notion that terminally ill patients ought to be able to end their lives, this did not mean that such a right existed or that it could be found in the Constitution.

Shortly after the Supreme Court had accepted the Washington and New York cases for review, Yale professor Stephen L. Carter published an article in the *New York Times Magazine* urging the courts not to, as he put it, "rush to lethal judgment." Carter saw the controversy over assisted suicide as above all a moral debate, and "except in emergencies, a court decision is the worst way to resolve a moral dilemma." If the courts decided this question, it would preempt a moral debate that had just begun; the courts should stay out of the issue and let the questions "be answered through popular debate and perhaps through legislation, not through legal briefs and litigation."

Carter believed that the judiciary had become involved too early, that there had not yet been a significant popular debate on the question. I suggest that by the time the courts of appeal heard these cases, popular debate had been going on for a number of years. Public opinion polls, popular referenda, books, articles in lay and scholarly journals, discussions on talk shows had made the question not only one that many Americans had thought about, but also one which they had reached some definite opinions as to how they, at least, wanted the issue resolved. The debate had certainly not ended, but given the fact that, as Tocqueville noted many years ago, "scarcely any political question arises in the United States that is not resolved, sooner or later, into a judicial question," it is neither surprising nor disturbing that assisted suicide had wound its way through the judicial labyrinth to the marble palace.

CHAPTER 7

The Supreme Court Decides

In recent years the Supreme Court has been fairly stingy in taking appeals from lower court decisions. Here one had a case of two circuits disagreeing, but they disagreed on the rationale for their findings, not on whether a right to physician-assisted suicide existed. Nonetheless, the Court granted certiorari to both cases at the very beginning of the October 1996 term.

The Court scheduled oral argument on the morning of January 8, 1997, and well before dawn protesters and people seeking tickets to hear the arguments gathered on the steps of the marble palace. Diane Coleman, the founder of the group Not Dead Yet, showed up in her wheelchair to protest the whole notion of physician-assisted suicide, while members of the Hemlock Society counterpicketed across the plaza. Bob Castagna, the executive director of the Oregon Catholic Conference, asked, "Will nature take its course, or will we turn doctors into angels of death?" Many of those in line had a more complex response to reporters' questions. Doris Kuehn's father had been a strong right-to-die proponent, and he had lost a lung and seven ribs because of tuberculosis. "I'm more pro than con," she said, "but you can't pin it down. Does it have to be severe pain, or is it just a feeling that I want to die? I know there are gray areas."

At ten o'clock the marshal called out the traditional "Oyez, oyez," and the nine justices filed in through the curtain to take their seats. Chief Justice Rehnquist called on Senior Assistant Attorney General William L. Williams to defend the Washington statute.

"We are here today," Williams declared, "representing the people of Washington to defend their legislative policy judgment to prohibit assisted suicide.... The issue here today is whether the Constitution requires the social policy developed by Washington voters must be supplanted by a far different social policy, a constitutionally recognized right to physician-assisted suicide that is contrary to our traditions."

Justice Ruth Bader Ginsburg began the questioning by noting that the Court's ruling in *Cruzan* recognized a liberty interest even while acknowledging the right of the state to regulate it. Why could not the Court do the same thing in this case, recognize a liberty interest and then give the states leeway to regulate it? Williams responded that recognizing a liberty interest would greatly limit the states' ability to regulate the problem. But if the Court did find a liberty interest, he believed the states' interests here were as strong as those the Court had recognized in *Cruzan*.

Justice Sandra Day O'Connor wanted to know what the state's interests would be if the Court decided to recognize a liberty interest in assisted suicide. Williams responded that the states were beginning to reassess where a line should be drawn, but that clearly the highest priority remained preserving life and preventing suicide; other important interests included prevention of abuse and undue influence, as well as regulation of the medical profession to protect patients.

The chief justice asked, "It would be very difficult to assume a liberty interest and rule in your favor in this case, would it not? Because if we assume a liberty interest but nonetheless say that, even assuming a liberty interest, a state can prohibit it entirely, that would be rather a conundrum."

Williams disagreed, trying to argue that the states' interests here was similar to those in *Cruzan,* but Rehnquist cut him off. In *Cruzan* the Court had dealt only with an evidentiary rule; here Washington wanted an outright prohibition.

Williams got no further than saying "That's correct" when Justice Antonin Scalia broke in. Wouldn't declaring a liberty interest be cost free, he wanted to know, if you immediately say it can be outweighed by the various social policies adopted by the states. Williams conceded the point, but noted that in *Oregon Employment Security Division v. Smith* (1990), the Court had supported an absolute ban on the use of peyote in the face of an even stronger individual interest, the First Amendment right to free exercise of religion.

The state contended that allowing assisted suicide to the terminally ill who wanted to end their lives raised the risk that the practice would expand to include those who did not want to hasten their deaths, as well as those not terminally ill. Justice David Souter asked a number of questions, wanting to know how realistic those fears were. "It's a plausible argument," he declared, "but how realistic is it? What method should I use [in evaluating the risk]? What basis is there to evaluate the claim that slippage will occur?"

Williams conceded that no empirical evidence existed in the American experience to assess the risk, but studies of the Netherlands indicated that acceptance of physician-assisted suicide had led to instances of involuntary euthanasia. Moreover, while proponents here claimed they wanted physician-assisted suicide in only a narrow class, he feared that if they won these cases, the next time around they would seek assisted suicide for a broader range of people and not just for the terminally ill.

Justice John Paul Stevens wanted to know whether states had the legislative authority to approve assisted suicide, and Williams agreed that they did. In response to a similar question on state power from Justice Anthony Kennedy, Williams noted that "if you accept a rational basis level of review, states have the maximum flexibility to decide on a state-by-state basis."

Where did one draw the line in actual practice? Justice Stevens asked. He knew of no instances where a doctor had ever been convicted for giving assistance in a suicide. Williams admitted he knew of no convictions, either. "But one assumes that there is a covert practice going on under current law and as the line gets muddier, the potential for abuse is much worse."

Williams then gave over the balance of his time to Acting United States Solicitor General Walter Dellinger, as the United States had filed an *amicus* brief on behalf of the states. Justice O'Connor immediately asked him how one could reconcile the government's position that a liberty interest existed but that the Washington State law should be upheld.

Dellinger responded that the interest involved was a liberty interest not in dying, but in avoiding severe pain, for which state law prevented certain patients from obtaining relief. While important, this did not rise to the level of a fundamental liberty interest such as the Court had found in *Cruzan,* namely, that the state cannot compel a person to continue unwanted medical treatment. "If the state is the only thing standing between you and pain relief," Dellinger said, "we think the person has a cognizable interest." But while "the individual stories [in appellants' briefs] are heartrending . . . it's important for this court to recognize that, if you were to affirm the judgment below, lethal medication could be proposed as a treatment, not just to those in severe pain, but to every competent terminally ill person in the country."

That has nothing to do with suicide, then, said Justice Antonin Scalia, nor with prohibitions against it. "What's critical," Dellinger argued, "is . . . if you affirm the judgments below, lethal medications could be prescribed as treatment for anyone."

"Now or ever," Justice Ginsburg interjected, "the case raises the basic issue of who decides. Is it ever a proper question for courts as opposed to the legislature to decide?"

Before Dellinger could answer, Justice Souter suggested that "maybe the Court should wait until it can know more."

Some studies existed, Dellinger answered, and they show it is possible to set up safeguards, "but the reality is that they can't be met" all the time. And in an ominous final comment, he noted that in a health care system attempting to treat pain and depression, lethal medication is the least costly treatment.

Kathryn L. Tucker of Seattle then rose to argue on behalf of the doctors and patients who had brought the suit. She defined the basic issue for her clients as whether patients on the threshold of death have a right to choose to end their lives with dignity.

Before she could go any further, Justice Scalia wanted to know why she would limit the right to such a small group, those "on the threshold," and why not to other patients, some of whom may be in pain for years.

Tucker responded that the only group for whom time is a critical element are those on the threshold, whose only real remaining choice is the manner of their imminent death. This is a relatively easy determination for a doctor to make. A person who still has potential for a fruitful life is not on that threshold; he or she has other choices.

Justice Ginsburg wanted to know how Tucker would deal with a person on the threshold of death whose pain was so severe that she could not herself administer the lethal drug, but would need a doctor's help.

Tucker avoided a direct answer here, because she knew that the medical associations who opposed physician-assisted suicide had hammered on the notion that doctors were supposed to save lives, not become executioners. She conceded that the state could impose a requirement of self-administration to ensure voluntariness, which she termed essential. The state could even impose a waiting period to ensure that the patient is making a reasoned decision. "We want the Court to find a protected right," she said, but also to allow experimentation on the state level.

Justices Rehnquist and Scalia then wanted Tucker to explain the difference between a liberty interest in refusing or withdrawing treatment and an interest in assisted suicide. In *Cruzan,* according to the chief justice, the Court had affirmed the right to refuse treatment, which merely carried on a right long embedded in common law. Rejecting treatment, Scalia interjected, is not the same as suicide. "Why can't society decide as a matter of public morality that it's wrong to kill yourself," just as it is wrong to kill another person?

Here Tucker had a ready answer. Assisted suicide in the circumstances of a terminally ill patient involves a very personal decision. It deals with one's own body and health care, not that of another person. The state may have a stronger interest in preserving life early on in the course of a person's illness, when that person still has a chance for a fruitful life. But the state's interest grows weaker as the person nears death, and it practically disappears when a person's only choice is how to die—not whether to live or die. Moreover, the state is inconsistent when it allows a person to make that choice in other circumstances, such as through advance directives.

As her time wound down, Tucker faced one final question from Justice O'Connor about the ability of a person to refuse life-sustaining treatment such as kidney dialysis. When Tucker responded that the state could intervene if that person had suicidal tendencies, Justice Scalia commented that her position would have to be broader than that if she truly wanted to leave decisions to individuals.

It took only a few minutes for the attorneys from the Washington case to leave the counsel tables and for those who would argue the New York case to take their place, and then the clerk called case number 95-1858, *Dennis C. Vacco, Attorney General of New York, et al. v. Timothy E. Quill et al.* Chief Justice Rehnquist invited Vacco to step to the podium and begin.

Vacco began by asserting that the New York law did not implicate any equal protection analysis because persons who declined medical treatment were not similarly situated to those who sought assistance in suicide. In withdrawal from treatment, death comes because of the underlying illness or condition; in suicide death comes from a deliberately administered lethal drug.

The legislature could draw the line where it wanted to, and in fact could permit assisted suicide. "We're here today to say it shouldn't be constitutionally compelled." The legislature had decided, through the law currently in effect, that allowing physician-assisted suicide could lead to euthanasia, a policy it did not want.

Justice Stevens asked Vacco whether the state could totally forbid the right to refuse treatment. "We'd be right back here," Vacco responded. He did not believe a legislature could constitutionally compel a dying person to continue treatment.

Scalia then wanted to know whether a state could authorize force-feeding for a person refusing treatment if that person was not at death's door. "Why limit the discretion of the legislature?" He noted the not uncommon practice of force-feeding a person who has gone on a hunger strike.

Vacco said he thought there was a big difference between force-feeding a person and violation of a person's bodily integrity through medication. This led the chief justice to note that "it seems odd that bodily integrity is not violated by sticking a spoon in your mouth but is by a needle in the arm."

It all depends, Vacco responded, on whether a person's intent is suicidal. While it was true that suicide was no longer a crime in New York, barriers to it still existed. The state-erected barriers were rational and had the legitimate purpose of preventing abuse.

Justice Ginsburg asked the attorney general to explain why he thought the Second Circuit had erred. He responded that the basic error lay in the lower court's equating people on life support who wished to terminate that treatment and people not on life support who wished to end their lives. These two groups are not similarly situated, and therefore an equal protection analysis did not apply. But, Ginsburg continued, the results are the same; one turns off a machine and dies, or one takes a pill and dies. There is a difference, the attorney general insisted. "It's rationally distinguishable because it is consistent medical practice.... Providing drugs specifically and solely for the purpose of killing someone has never been embraced by the medical profession."

Justice Souter then engaged in a fairly lengthy exchange with Vacco over the difference between giving medication for pain relief that might, incidentally, lead to death and giving the same medication for the express purpose of causing death. To justify this distinction, the justice noted, one had to differentiate between people on life support, who had a right to end treatment and therefore could be overmedicated to alleviate pain, and those not on life support. Isn't the line one of abuse?

Exactly, Vacco agreed. "The principal . . . justification indeed, one of the most compelling reasons, state interest, is the risk of abuse." While a risk of abuse existed in the treatment of patients going off life support, the state considered the risk far greater for the terminally ill not on life support.

Acting Solicitor General Dellinger then returned to the lectern and in a nutshell summarized the essence of the Second

Circuit argument: "if the state may, as a general matter, legitimately prohibit the granting of lethal medication, the fact that these states permit practices that are in the respondents' view medically, ethically, and morally indistinguishable from lethal medication requires that these states also do that." Dellinger said the United States disagreed with that view and, like Vacco, believed a common-sense distinction could be drawn between the two groups. "The historic distinction between killing someone and letting them die is so powerful that we believe it fully suffices here."

Justice Ginsburg asked the solicitor general if he could deal with what she termed the "winks and nods" argument, that the issue constituted a great sham because doctors had historically provided suicide assistance for "anybody who is sophisticated enough to want it." Dellinger denied that any evidentiary practice existed to support this claim.

When Harvard Law School professor Laurence H. Tribe rose to support the case for physician-assisted suicide, he immediately attacked as a "fantasy" the notion that "at the end you're either in this closed class of people who luckily have a plug that can be pulled or you're in some other group." When Justice Kennedy noted a historic common law distinction, Tribe tried to pull the justices into the real world. "None of these patients is in a state of nature. They're in a hospital or a hospice." The state certainly has a right to characterize certain actions as suicide, but "the government's characterizations can't control our constitutional analysis."

Tribe took what appears on paper at least to be a fairly belligerent view. He called the alleged difference between patients on life support and others terminally ill a fantasy. He agreed that the states could differ in how they wanted to deal with the problem, that they could serve, in Justice Brandeis's words, as laboratories for experimentation. But "these laboratories are now operating largely with the lights out. They're operating with the lights out because it's not just New York." They had combined two principles, and in their doing so the whole logic of opposition to physician-assisted suicide collapsed.

One principle allows a physician to medicate to reduce pain, even if it will hasten death—providing that death is "not your real intent." The other principle permits a patient to refuse treatment or have treatment terminated. The result is overmedication, allegedly to kill pain but in reality to hasten death. This "terminal sedation," as he called it, "is overwhelmingly documented everywhere in the country, it's not some sneaky practice."

Tribe also gave what may have been the best definition of the claimed liberty interest in response to a question from Justice Stevens:

> The liberty interest in this case is the liberty, when facing imminent and inevitable death, not to be forced by the government to endure a degree of pain and suffering that one can relieve only by being completely unconscious. Not to be forced into that choice, that the liberty is the freedom, at this threshold at the end of life, not to be a creature of the state but to have some voice in the question of how much pain one is really going through.

———

The justices handed down their decisions in the two cases on June 26, 1997, at the very end of the term. Their finding, that the Constitution did not provide a right to physician-assisted suicide, did not surprise anyone, although the fact that all nine agreed on the holding may have raised a few eyebrows. But three of the four justices in *Cruzan* who would have found a stronger liberty interest—Brennan, Marshall, and Blackmun—had left the bench, and the centrists who had taken their place shared the view that the Court had to be careful in finding new rights. As in *Cruzan,* Chief Justice Rehnquist delivered the Court's opinions.

In *Washington v. Glucksberg,* the Court rejected the Ninth Circuit's claim that physician-assisted suicide constituted a fundamental liberty interest protected by the Due Process Clause. Rehnquist began, "as we do in all due-process cases, by examining our Nation's history, legal traditions, and practices." The history and tradition yielded no support that assistance in suicide had ever been considered a personal right, and "for over 700 years, the Anglo-American common-law tradition has punished or otherwise disapproved of both suicide and assisting suicide." Although in recent years there had been a trend away from the common law's harsh sanctions, this reflected not an acceptance of suicide but rather a belief that the suicide's family should not be punished for his wrongdoing. As for assisting suicide, the various states had in recent years reexamined and generally reaffirmed the ban.

But individuals now die primarily in institutions such as hospitals and nursing homes, and "public concern and democratic action are therefore sharply focused on how best to protect dignity and independence at the end of life, with the result that there have been many significant changes in state laws and the attitudes these laws reflect." Nonetheless, "despite changes in medical technology and not withstanding an increased emphasis on the importance of end-of-life decisionmaking, we have not retreated from this prohibition" on assisted suicide. Having recited this historical antipathy toward assisted suicide, the chief justice turned to the constitutional claims.

He began by agreeing that the Due Process Clause protects more than fair process and said the liberty "it protects includes more than the absence of physical restraint." He ticked off a long list of cases in which the Court had found fundamental rights and interests, but "we 'have always been reluctant to expand the concept of substantive due process because guideposts for responsible decisionmaking in this area are scarce and open-ended.'" The Court's established due process analysis involved determining whether the claimed liberty interest is "deeply rooted in this Nation's history and tradition" and whether there is a "careful description" of the asserted liberty interest.

Did the asserted interest in assisted suicide have any place in the nation's traditions? The answer could only be in the negative. "To hold for respondents, we would have to reverse centuries of legal doctrine and practice, and strike down the considered policy choice of almost every State."

In the second part of the analysis, the need for "careful description," the Court also rejected the respondents' claim that the liberty interest in assisted suicide should be seen as consistent with the Court's long line of due process decisions enumerating rights protected under the Fourteenth Amendment. Here the chief justice went to great pains to declare what the Court had said and had not said in the two cases relied upon in the Ninth Circuit, *Casey* and *Cruzan*.

In the latter case, the Court had indeed held that a right existed to terminate life-sustaining treatment, but it had also upheld the state's right to require clear and convincing evidence, especially in the case of an incompetent, of what the patient really wanted. In doing so, Rehnquist noted, the Court did not deduce a right "from abstract concepts of personal autonomy." Rather, there existed a long common law tradition that treated forced medication as a battery and that upheld a person's right to refuse unwanted medical treatment. That is all the Court said, "and we certainly gave no intimation that the right to refuse unwanted medical treatment could be somehow transmuted into a right to assistance in committing suicide."

As for *Casey,* the Court there had concluded that "the essential holding of *Roe v. Wade* should be retained and once again reaffirmed." The case dealt with abortion, but it did note that many of the rights and liberties subsumed under due process "involved the most intimate and personal choices a person may make in a lifetime." But the lower courts had gone too far and had read this phrase to mean far more than the Court had intended. The Court had summed up rights it had already found and had not issued a formula for identifying new rights. "That many of the rights and liberties protected by the Due Process Clause sound in personal autonomy does not warrant the sweeping conclusion that any and all important, intimate, and personal decisions are so protected."

Rehnquist then went into an extended analysis of the state's interest in preventing suicide, and found all of them convincing—preservation of human life, protection of the integrity of the medical profession, protection of vulnerable groups such as the poor and the elderly, and fear of a slippery slope, with assisted suicide leading to voluntary and perhaps even involuntary euthanasia. The Court found that all of these interests are legitimate and that "Washington's ban on assisted suicide is at least reasonably related to their promotion and protection."

In conclusion, the Court reversed the *en banc* decision of the Court of Appeals, but the chief justice noted that "throughout the Nation, Americans are engaged in an earnest and profound debate about the morality, legality, and practicality of physician-assisted suicide. Our holding permits this debate to continue, as it should in a democratic society." Despite the fact that states had traditionally opposed assisted suicide, nothing in the Court's opinion was intended to foreclose them from changing their minds. The decision followed almost precisely the prescription that Professor Sunstein had endorsed, an opinion that did not constitutionalize a right to assisted suicide, did not foreclose that as an option for the states, and did urge a continuation of the democratic dialogue.

———

In the companion case of *Vacco v. Quill,* Rehnquist took less than seven pages to overturn the Second Circuit, in part because he did not find it necessary to reiterate his lengthy historical analysis from the Ninth Circuit opinion. He began his analysis by noting that facially, New York's ban on assisted suicide and its statutes permitting patients to refuse life-sustaining treatment do not "treat anyone differently than anyone else or draw any distinctions between persons. *Everyone,* regardless of physical condition, is entitled, if competent, to refuse unwanted lifesaving medical treatment; *no one* is permitted to assist a suicide." In general, according to the chief justice, "laws that apply evenhandedly to all 'unquestionably comply' with the Equal Protection Clause."

The Second Circuit had based its opinion on the conclusion that people who were refused physician-assisted suicide stood in the same position as those on life-sustaining equipment and that by allowing one group to hasten death yet denying this to the other, the state violated the strictures of the Equal Protection Clause. The high court, however, disagreed completely with this analysis. "Unlike the Court of Appeals, we think the distinction between assisting suicide and withdrawing life-sustaining treatment, a distinction widely recognized and endorsed in the medical profession and in our legal traditions, is both important and logical; it is certainly rational."

The Court found legal justification in the "fundamental legal principles of causation and intent." If a patient declines treatment, he dies from the underlying cause; if he takes a lethal dosage of a drug, he is killed by that action. As to the purported claim that there is no difference between a doctor's honoring a patient's wishes to have treatment terminated and giving a patient a lethal overdose, the Court found that in the former instance the physician is respecting his patient's request and "ceases doing useless and futile or degrading things to the patient when [the patient] no longer stands to benefit from them." Even when a patient dies from "aggressive palliative care," the intent of the doctor is to alleviate the pain, not to kill the patient. But the physician who assists a suicide "must, necessarily and indubitably, intend primarily that the patient be made dead."

The chief justice did not think this distinction a difficult one, and in fact a number of state courts had clearly distinguished one from the other. Looking to the most famous of the lower court assisted-suicide cases, that of Dr. Jack Kevorkian, Rehnquist noted that the Michigan Supreme Court "also rejected the argument that the distinction 'between acts that artificially sustain life and acts that artificially curtail life' is merely a 'distinction without constitutional significance—a meaningless exercise in semantic gymnastics,' insisting that the 'Cruzan majority disagreed and so do we.'" Similarly, state legislatures had had no difficulty understanding the difference, and had written that distinction into law.

Contrary to claims of the petitioners, New York had not written an irrational or idiosyncratic bias into its law; rather, the legislature had prudently deliberated, held numerous hearings, and mandated studies. It had carefully delineated patients' rights while defining the interests of the state, and in doing so had reaffirmed what it saw as a clear line between "letting die" and "killing." In this the Court's ruling in *Cruzan* had been misinterpreted below, since in that case the majority had "recognized, at least implicitly, the distinction between letting a patient die and making that patient die." *Cruzan*, the chief justice emphasized, "provides no support for the notion that refusing life-sustaining medical treatment is 'nothing more nor less than suicide.'"

Since logic and practice supported New York's judgment that a clear and important distinction existed between allowing a patient to die and making that patient die, the state could therefore treat these two groups of patients differently without violating the Constitution. In conclusion, the chief justice reiterated what he saw as important state interests—prohibiting intentional killing; preserving life; protecting the role of physician as healer; sheltering vulnerable people from abuse, prejudice, and financial pressure to end their lives; and "avoiding a possible slide toward euthanasia"—all discussed in *Glucksberg*. "These valid and important public interests easily satisfy the constitutional requirement that a legislative classification bear a rational relation to some legitimate end."

The concurring opinions are far more interesting and nuanced than the majority decisions, in which the chief justice took a straightforward and rather simplistic approach. In reversing the Ninth Circuit's finding of a liberty interest in *Glucksberg*, Rehnquist appealed to history to show that suicide had always been disfavored and that even after the states had repealed their laws criminalizing self-murder, they had kept on the books those laws prohibiting assistance in suicide. Neither history nor contemporary developments had ever created a liberty interest that demanded the state permit physician-assisted suicide, and the Ninth Circuit had totally misread the key cases of *Casey* and

Cruzan in reaching its decision. In *Vacco v. Quill,* the majority had denied that the Equal Protection Clause demanded that states treated terminally ill patients the same as those on life-support systems; it emphatically rejected the idea that allowing the latter to die equated with helping the former to their deaths. Advocates of assisted suicide could draw little hope from the majority opinions other than that the Court had not barred a state from permitting physician-assisted suicide.

Justice David Souter wrote an eighteen-page concurrence to *Glucksberg,* in which he carefully explored the history of substantive due process, from its beginnings in the early days of the Republic to its repudiation after its abuse by conservatives attacking economic regulation. But Souter also noted that substantive due process had been used to defend individual liberties as well as property rights, and here he clearly considered Justice John Marshall Harlan's dissent in *Poe v. Ullman* (1961) the most important statement of the type of rights subsumed within due process. Souter found three elements of that opinion necessary to any analysis of Fourteenth Amendment liberty interests. First, he noted Harlan's "respect for the tradition of substantive due process review" and the necessity for the courts to undertake that review. "For two centuries American courts," Souter noted, "and for much of that time this Court, have thought it necessary to provide some degree of review over the substantive content of legislation under constitutional standards of textual breadth." Harlan saw due process as far more than procedural correctness. "Were due process merely a procedural safeguard," Harlan had written, "it would fail to reach those situations where the deprivation of life, liberty or property was accomplished by legislation which by operating in the future could, given the fairest possible procedure in application to individuals, nevertheless destroy the enjoyment of all three." Therefore, Souter concluded, the very text of the Due Process Clause imposes on the courts "nothing less than an obligation to give substantive content to the words 'liberty' and 'due process of law.' "

Harlan's second point in *Poe* reminded the Court that the purpose of such review "is not the identification of extratextual

absolutes but scrutiny of a legislative resolution (perhaps unconscious) of clashing principles, each quite possibly worthy in and
of itself, but each to be weighed within the history of our values
as a people." The court weighs the strengths of opposing claims
and does not substitute its judgment based on what justices see
as first premises. Thus, even if the judges personally prefer one
form of resolution over another, they cannot substitute their
judgment for that of the legislature, unless that body has ex-
ceeded clear constitutional parameters. This leads to Harlan's
third point, the necessity to pay attention to detail as an element
no less essential than understanding the positions of the competing sides or recognizing the extent of legislative judgment.

Souter went into this extended buildup, I believe, because he
found the majority opinion devoid of compassion or awareness
of the claims of terminally ill patients. The majority had found
no historic basis for recognizing assisted suicide as a liberty
interest, and therefore no liberty interest existed. Souter understood that due process had been used in the past to create or at
least to recognize hitherto latent rights. While not ready to
create a right to assisted suicide, he wanted to acknowledge that
even if the legislature had been well within its powers to make
the choice it did, and even if judicial deference required the
courts to respect that decision, those seeking the right also had
a claim that the courts needed to hear even if they did not agree
with it. Souter also implied that the majority had been far too
rigid in its analysis, and he quoted from Harlan in *Poe,* as well
as Justice Lewis Powell, that appropriate review of substantive
due process claims comes not from drawing arbitrary lines but
from understanding the historic bases of those claims as well as
the recognition of shared social values.

Courts, according to Souter, had "to assess the relative
'weights' or dignities of the contending interests, and to this
extent the judicial method is familiar to the common law." But
in doing so, courts had to be careful to confine any liberty
interests they recognized to those that truly deserved constitutional stature, those "so rooted in the traditions and conscience
of our people as to be ranked as fundamental." Courts also had

to remember that their business involved constitutional review, not judicial lawmaking. Thus judges had to review the competing claims carefully with great attention to detail, but they had no right to substitute their preferences for those of the legislative branch. Justice Harlan had set clear standards for courts to follow in due process review, a path that on the one hand avoided the arbitrariness of absolutes and on the other stood firm against making simple reasonableness a standard for declaring rights.

With these standards in mind, Souter now turned to the question before the Court. Unlike the majority, Souter framed the question in very limited terms. "Here we are faced with an individual claim not to a right on the part of just anyone to help anyone else commit suicide under any circumstances, but to the right of a narrow class to help others also in a narrow class under a set of limited circumstances." To this claim, the state responds "that rights of such narrow scope cannot be recognized without jeopardy to individuals whom the State may concededly protect through its regulations."

Souter's analysis of the patients' and doctors' claim showed far greater sensitivity to nuance than did the majority opinion. The respondents did not base their claim on history, but in fact acknowledged that historically there had been prohibitions. The lesson of history was not that suicide had at one time been considered a criminal act, but rather that it had long since been decriminalized. But Souter refused to follow the respondents' argument that this opened the door to requiring the decriminalization of assisting in suicide. The reasons for decriminalization may have had far more to do with the practical ability of the state to prevent such acts than any change in popular moral views. "Thus it may indeed make sense for the State to take its hands off suicide as such, while continuing to prohibit the sort of assistance that would make its commission easier." Decriminalization by itself did not imply the existence of any constitutional right or liberty interest.

Both the Ninth Circuit and the respondents had made much of the Court's analysis of bodily autonomy in *Casey*, and Souter acknowledged that analogies existed between the abortion cases and those dealing with assisted suicide—most important, the need for a doctor in both instances. Without a doctor's assistance in abortion, "the woman's right would have too often amounted to nothing more than a right to self-mutilation, and without a physician to assist in the suicide of the dying, the patient's right will often be confined to crude methods of causing death, most shocking and painful to the decedent's survivors."

Souter also agreed that one could make a strong case that physician-assisted suicide fell within "the accepted tradition of medical care in our society." In the abortion cases the Court recognized the need for a doctor, and not just to perform the medical procedure. The Court "recognized that the good physician is not just a mechanic of the human body whose services have no bearing on a person's moral choices, but one who does more than treat symptoms, one who ministers to the patient." The idea of the physician treating the whole person is just as important in end-of-life decisions as in abortion. The patients in this case wanted not only an end to their pain (which Souter noted they might have had, although only at the price of stupor), "but an end to their short remaining lives with a dignity that they believed would be denied them by powerful pain medication, as well as by their consciousness of dependency and helplessness as they approached death." One could hardly imagine any other circumstances in which the call for bodily autonomy carried greater weight and in which the role of the physician, including assistance, fell within the "traditional norm" of health care. In fact, the State had already recognized this right in its willingness to allow terminally ill patients to stop treatment and to withdraw life-sustaining medication, thus hastening death. It even allowed physicians to administer powerful painkilling medication in this terminal condition, even if such dosages brought on death.

Up until this point one might have thought Souter to be preparing a dissent rather than a concurrence. He summed up the respondents' arguments as going through "three steps of increasing forcefulness." First, suicide had been decriminalized; second, decriminalization provided freedom of choices analogous to individual options in recognized areas of bodily autonomy, such as abortion; and third, the claim for assistance is based not on some broad principle but rather on the traditional role of doctors in ministering to all the medical needs of their patients. Souter found this a powerful argument, one demanding, under the *Poe* criteria, "careful scrutiny of the State's contrary claim."

Souter then proceeded to do just that. The State had essentially put forward three interests to justify its law—protecting life generally, discouraging suicide (even if knowing and voluntary), and protecting terminally ill patients from involuntary suicide or from euthanasia. Souter found it unnecessary to discuss the first two, since the third argument proved dispositive for him. The State had argued that a very slippery slope existed and that it would be all too easy, perhaps inevitable, to progress down that slope. Souter summarized the argument as follows:

> Mistaken decisions may result from inadequate palliative care or a terminal prognosis that turns out to be error; coercion and abuse may stem from the large medical bills that family members cannot bear or unreimbursed hospitals decline to shoulder. Voluntary and involuntary euthanasia may result once doctors are authorized to prescribe lethal medication in the first instance, for they might find it pointless to distinguish between patients who administer their own fatal drugs and those who wish not to, and their compassion for those who suffer may obscure the distinction between those who ask for death and those who may be unable to request it.

Here, unlike in the majority opinion, is found not only the suffering of the individual patient, but also the concerns of a compassionate state. The chief justice had found the state interests to be rational and history to be opposed to assisted suicide; there was barely a hint of the individual, patient or doctor, all of whom had to live within this system with no recourse. Souter seemed to imply that should conditions change, the Court might also reconsider.

The example of the Netherlands had been invoked by both sides, the respondents to support their claim that strong rules would prevent abuse, the state to allege that euthanasia had gotten out of control. Souter took the middle route, and the one supported by the bulk of the evidence, namely, that "a substantial dispute" existed about what the Dutch experience meant. While that dispute might someday be resolved, until then there existed enough evidence to support the State's concern about legitimizing assisted suicide. "The day may come when we can say with some assurance which side is right [in what the Dutch practice means], but for now it is the substantiality of the factual disagreement, and the alternatives for resolving it, that matter. They are, for me, dispositive of the due process claim *at this time.*"

Given this dispute, Souter would defer to the legislative judgment, but he added that much remained to be learned on the subject. For the moment the legislature was as well suited as the judiciary to undertake that examination. Moreover, in declaring constitutional rights courts ought to act with finality and cannot experiment with what might or might not be done under differing circumstances.

"Legislatures, however, are not so constrained. The experimentation that should be out of the question in constitutional adjudication displacing legislative judgment is entirely proper, as well as highly desirable, when the legislative power addresses an emerging issue like assisted suicide. . . . *While I do not decide for all time that respondents' claim should not be recognized,* I acknowledge the legislative institutional competence as the better one to deal with that claim at this time."

Souter's is a far better opinion than that of the majority. The Rehnquist opinion is rigid and formulistic, with barely a hint of the great emotional issues involved, the pain and suffering of individuals and their families, the moral dilemmas of doctors, the effect on society. Souter is cognizant of these matters, and if he cannot give those in pain the answer they want, he at least acknowledges that they have a legitimate claim, that mere recourse to history is an evasion rather than an answer. And he clearly leaves the door open for the Court to revisit this matter, even as he urges the states to grapple further with it.

Justice Sandra Day O'Connor, the only justice to file a concurrence who also signed onto the Court's opinion, also implied that given another set of factual circumstances and claims, she too would be willing to reconsider the decision. The majority had framed the issue fairly narrowly, namely whether the Due Process Clause protects a right to commit suicide that includes the right to have assistance in doing so, and then concluded that the nation's history and legal traditions did not support such a right. With this she agreed, namely, "that there is no generalized right to 'commit suicide.'" Respondents, however, had asked the Court to address a narrower question: Does a mentally competent person experiencing great pain and suffering have a constitutionally protected right to control the circumstances of his or her imminent death?

This claim need not be reached in either case, O'Connor noted, because such people could already get the relief they sought. "The parties and amici agree that in these States a patient who is suffering from terminal illness and who is experiencing great pain has no legal barriers to obtaining medication, from qualified physicians, to alleviate that suffering, even to the point of causing unconsciousness and hastening death." Given this fact, then, she saw no reason why the state should not be allowed to pursue its legitimate interests in protecting those who were not truly competent or whose decisions might not be truly voluntary.

O'Connor left unsaid what she would do were the states to change that situation. What might happen should the states, in their efforts to protect those needing protection, impinge upon the ability of the competent to gain this relief? She urged the states to continue in their "extensive and serious evaluation of physician-assisted suicide and other related issues," because "every one of us at some point may be affected by our own or a family member's terminal illness."

Justice Ruth Bader Ginsberg noted briefly that she concurred in the judgments in the two cases "substantially for the reasons stated by Justice O'Connor in her concurring opinion." Justice

Stephen Breyer also joined in O'Connor's concurrence, but not insofar as it joined in the majority reasoning. Breyer went on to explain that in *Vacco* he agreed that the state interests justified differentiating between physician-assisted suicide and withdrawal of life support, and he also agreed with the majority that no liberty interest existed under the Fourteenth Amendment to support the respondents' claim. But he differed with the Court on how it formulated that right, namely, a right to commit suicide with another's assistance. Breyer said he would not reject the claim without considering a different formulation, which might have greater support within the American legal tradition. "That formulation would use words roughly like a 'right to die with dignity.' But irrespective of the exact words used, at its core would lie personal control over the manner of death, professional medical assistance, and the avoidance of unnecessary and severe physical suffering—combined."

Breyer referred to Souter's due process analysis, and like him, did not believe "that this Court need or now should decide whether or not such a right [to die with dignity] is 'fundamental.'" The avoidance of severe physical pain would be essential to such a claim, and as Justice O'Connor had pointed out, the laws of New York and Washington did not force a dying person to undergo that pain. Doctors could prescribe palliative medication, even to the point of hastening death. Thus state law did not infringe upon a central interest the way that anticontraceptive laws had done in *Poe* or *Griswold*. But

> were the legal circumstances different—for example, were state laws to prevent the provision of palliative care, including the administration of drugs as needed to avoid pain at the end of life—then the law's impact upon serious and otherwise un-avoidable physical pain (accompanying death) would be more directly at issue. And as Justice O'Connor suggests, the Court might have to revisit its conclusions in these cases.

The lone member of the *Cruzan* minority still sitting on the Court, John Paul Stevens, also concurred in the judgment. The majority had noted that its holding remained consistent with the ongoing debate over the morality, legality, and practicality of physician-assisted suicide; Stevens wrote separately "to make it clear that there is also room for further debate about the limits that the Constitution places on the power of the States to punish the practice."

The respondents had filed a facial challenge to the laws, and while the Court has not always been clear on what criteria are to be used in evaluating a facial challenge, in general plaintiffs have to show a broader violation of constitutional rights than they would in an "as applied" challenge, in which the statute's constitutionality is challenged as applied to a particular plaintiff or group of plaintiffs. Facial challenges are the most difficult, "since the challenger must establish that no set of circumstances exists under which the Act would be valid." Referring to the Court's previous decisions in capital punishment cases, Stevens noted that

> just as our conclusion that capital punishment is not always unconstitutional did not preclude later decisions holding that it is sometimes impermissibly cruel, so it is equally clear that a decision upholding a general statutory prohibition of assisted suicide does not mean that every possible application of the statute would be valid. A State, like Washington, that has authorized the death penalty and thereby has concluded that the sanctity of human life does not require that it always be preserved, must acknowledge that there are situations in which an interest in hastening death is legitimate. Indeed, not only is that interest sometimes legitimate, *I am also convinced that there are times when it is entitled to constitutional protection.*

Stevens referred to *Cruzan,* which had been used by both circuit courts to justify their decisions and which Rehnquist claimed had been misinterpreted. The majority in that case had agreed that a liberty interest existed but that it might be outweighed by relevant state interests. Stevens agreed, but believed that Nancy Cruzan's right went beyond a common law rule. "Rather, this right is an aspect of a far broader and more basic concept of freedom that is even older than the common law. This freedom embraces, not merely a person's right to refuse a particular kind of unwanted treatment, but also her interest in dignity, and in determining the character of the memories that will survive long after her death." The majority in *Cruzan*, he believed, implicitly recognized that right.

Cruzan also meant that some state intrusions on how individuals choose to encounter death would not be tolerated. The original patients, now dead, in the Washington and New York cases "may in fact have had a liberty interest even stronger than Nancy Cruzan's because, not only were they terminally ill, they were suffering constant and severe pain." Stevens denied any absolute right to physician-assisted suicide, but he believed that *Cruzan* meant that people who no longer had a choice in whether to live or die, because they were already at death's door, had "a constitutionally protected interest that may outweigh the State's interest in preserving life at all costs." Stevens believed that in such situations, the liberty interest was different from and far stronger than the common law rule and also trumped any state interest. "It is an interest in deciding how, rather than whether, a critical threshold shall be crossed."

Stevens concurred in the New York case because he did believe a difference existed between letting someone die and hastening that person's death, and in the Washington case because he did not think a broad liberty interest existed. But he, like Souter, O'Connor, Ginsberg, and Breyer, did not believe the issue definitively resolved. Like them, he also encouraged the states to experiment and explore the issue further.

Epilogue

What is one to make of this plethora of opinions? First, it is clear that the case involved far more than considerations of constitutional interpretation. The Court's decision in *Cruzan* earlier in the decade had elicited little negative comment, since most Americans believe that people on life support should have the choice of refusing treatment, and a long line of common law cases confirmed the legal rationale for supporting that choice. In addition, medical and religious groups then and now do not equate the cessation of treatment with suicide, on the grounds that the underlying illness or condition is the actual cause of death. But popular attitudes toward suicide are quite diverse; there is no consensus on whether people have a "right" to kill themselves, much less on whether others should be permitted to help them. While doctors covertly provide prescriptions for lethal dosages of medication, the medical profession as a whole is on record as opposed to legalizing physician-assisted suicide. Aware of the lack of a popular concensus, the Court did not want to get out ahead of public opinion and call down upon itself the same firestorm of criticism that had greeted its decision in *Roe v. Wade*. The justices have wisely allowed the debate to continue but have left themselves the option, if needed, of revisiting the issue. From the viewpoint of judicial politics, the Court reached the "right" decision in the two cases.

But what about the issues in these cases? Has the Court provided any guidance other than allowing the states great leeway in what they choose to do? The chief justice's opinions in the two cases are extremely formalistic, and while they pay lip service to the fact that end-of-life decisions may be emotionally distressing, one finds very little compassion in his analysis. In essence, the majority utilized a test for determining liberty interests that is both simple and simplistic: "Is there a historic basis for such an interest? If yes, then we are willing to grant it some level of constitutional recognition. If no, then there is no right, and the states are free to ignore the claim."

While that is attractive, in that such a test provides a relatively straightforward analytic scheme, it also ignores the fact that the world we live in is not the world of 1789 nor that of 1868. We inhabit a world of automobiles, airplanes, telephones, computers, and medical sophistication undreamed of at the framing of the Constitution and the Fourteenth Amendment. To insist on interpreting the Due Process Clause of the Fourteenth Amendment as if nothing has happened in the last 130 years is to put the Constitution into a straitjacket. As Judge Reinhard noted in his opinion for the Ninth Circuit, were history the sole guide for interpreting the Fourteenth Amendment, then the Court could never have overturned the antimiscegenation statutes.

Over the Court's long history majority opinions have often been overshadowed and even replaced by concurring or dissenting opinions. In the assisted-suicide cases, Justice Souter's concurrence may well become the opinion that lower courts look to for future guidance. His elucidation of Justice Harlan's dissent in *Poe v. Ullman* not only is a more persuasive argument for how one determines when a liberty interest is implicated, but also is far better constitutional analysis. Souter recognized, as did the other justices who refused to sign on to the Rehnquist opinions, that end-of-life issues will become increasingly important in American society. Merely stating that they were not an issue in 1868 is neither going to serve as a guide to lower courts nor provide much comfort to Americans who will have to wrestle with these issues on a personal basis.

The critical issue is to what extent a democratic society is willing to grant individual autonomy to people who will then use that autonomy to make decisions with which a majority may not agree. American democracy has been unique not only in that it has relied on faith in the people as a whole to govern themselves, but also in the great latitude it has given individuals to choose how to lead their own lives. There are some critics who believe that we have allowed this individualistic strain to grow too large, overbalancing the needed sense of community that keeps society in balance. But surely the lower courts were right in their view that end-of-life choices, like abortion, involve "the most intimate and personal choices a person may make in a lifetime, choices central to personal dignity and autonomy, and [therefore] central to the liberty protected by the Fourteenth Amendment."

Moreover, the reasoning of many judges and ethicists, as well as various medical groups, regarding the distinction between terminating life support and taking an overdose of lethal medication strikes some as spurious. The conscious, competent person who turns off a ventilator or who stops going to dialysis sessions knows what the result will be, as does the conscious, competent person who washes down one hundred Seconal pills with vodka. If the second person is suffering from a painful and incurable illness, but is not on life support, why shouldn't she have the same option as the first person, to end a life that has lost meaning and contains nothing but pain and suffering? This was the lesson Lawrence Tribe tried to teach the justices, that in the real world people who are suffering but not on life support are still suffering; why should they be treated differently from those on life support who have the choice of ending their misery?

One of the more disturbing features of the Court's decision is the fact that the justices seemed aware of the fact that doctors do, every day, help patients to die and that they appeared willing to allow this practice to continue in a form of gray market. Mark Graber, in his book on abortion, has described a gray market as a quasi-legal arrangement whereby governmental authorities acquiesce and sometimes even aid in the distribution of goods or services that nominally are forbidden to all. Under the guise of "pain relief" authorities will allow a doctor to prescribe opiates in lethal dosages, in the fiction that all the physician is trying to do is ease the suffering, and that should death occur, it would be an unintended by-product. The result of continuing this practice will be that middle- and upper-middle-class people who have access to the health care system and are sophisticated about how it works will be able to exercise individual autonomy in their end-of-life choices. Others without such access and knowledge will have no control over their deaths.

What about the moral arguments? What about people who believe that suicide, even for those who are terminally ill and suffering, is an affront to God? These people have every right not to commit suicide, just as women who do not believe in abortion have every right not to have one. In fact, the case here is even stronger than in the abortion debate. Opponents of abortion say they are defending the life and the rights of the unborn who are powerless to protect themselves. But end-of-life decisions involve no innocent, mute, and powerless third parties, just the man or woman who wants to end his or her torment. As for physicians who do not want to participate in such a practice, they also have a choice. No one is forcing them to prescribe lethal overdoses, just as doctors are not forced to perform abortions against their will.

A stronger argument deals with protecting the vulnerable — the poor, the elderly, the less than fully competent — who may be under pressure from their family to end it all and to stop being a financial and emotional burden on their loved ones. This is a legitimate interest of the state, and no one in favor of assisted suicide believes it should be anything other than a voluntary choice free from undue pressure. There is a slippery slope, but stringent and effective regulations could be put into place to ensure that the option of physician-assisted suicide is not abused and misused. The law, as Ronald Dworkin has argued, must protect people "who think it would be appalling to be killed, even if they had only painful minutes to live. But the law must also protect those with the opposite conviction: that it would be appalling not to be offered an easier, calmer death with the help of doctors they trust."

Nor should one ignore the fact that end-of-life treatment for many people is terribly bad, often little more than a warehousing of the sick and infirm until they die. One reason Michigan prosecutors could not get a conviction of Jack Kevorkian in his three trials for assisting suicide is that the jurors saw his "Mercy Machine" as the only available option to weeks or months of suffering under horrible conditions. Opponents of assisted suicide recognize this problem and are calling for better treatment of the terminally ill rather than for an easy fix of euthanasia. In an ideal world, there would be a range of options that would include good hospital treatment for the terminally ill, effective pain management, and hospice care, as well as physician-assisted suicide. The debate should not be allowed to become one of all or nothing, suicide or suffering.

For the time being, the Court, despite the unconvincing opinion of the chief justice, has done the right thing. One needs to keep in mind that the whole question of right to die is a relatively new one and that of assisted suicide even newer. There is a national debate going on, and it should be allowed to continue uninterrupted. The closeness of the initiative votes in Washington and California and the passage of Measure 16 in Oregon indicate that a large number of Americans want to have the option of controlling their own end-of-life choices.

Attention will now be focused on the Oregon experience, to see if a program can be effective in giving some people the choice they want without its being abused by others. Many years ago Justice Brandeis wrote that "it is one of the happy incidents of the federal system that a single courageous State may, if its citizens choose, serve as a laboratory, and try novel social and economic experiments without risk to the rest of the country." That experiment has begun. On March 24, 1998, a woman in her mid-eighties became the first person in Oregon to commit suicide with the legal assistance of a doctor. The woman, whose identity is kept secret under terms of the state law, suffered from breast cancer and, according to her doctor, had less than two months to live. She had been having increasing difficulty in breathing and could no longer enjoy the simple pleasures that had meant so much to her, such as gardening. Hannah Davidson, with the Oregon Death With Dignity Legal Defense and

Education Fund, noted that a death is not a reason to celebrate, "but it is good for us. It was a personal decision, and it showed that the law worked." Opponents predictably denounced the event. Gayle Atteberry, executive director of Oregon Right to Life, issued a statement that "This marks the first day in history when a society sits idly by and lets someone kill themselves with the help of a doctor." Oregon medical groups did not comment.

Predictions that Oregon would become a beacon for the suicidal, or start the nation down the slippery slope to mass death, have not materialized. In fact, relatively few people have exercised their rights under this law. At the end of August 1998, ten months after the law went into effect, only eight people had died from lethal drugs prescribed by a physician. Two others had secured prescriptions, but succumbed to their illness before using the medication. Nine of the ten suffered from cancer, and the other had heart problems. There were five men and five women, with an average age of 71.

While these numbers will in all likelihood rise in the future, the initial figures indicate that Oregonians, like the Dutch, are in no rush to kill themselves and will make judicious use of their rights under the death-with-dignity law. Proponents of physician-assisted suicide have never argued that all sick and elderly patients, or all people suffering from a debilitating terminal disease, should commit suicide. Rather, they have argued that there should be choices available and that physician-assisted suicide should be one of those choices.

One cannot predict how the Oregon experiment will proceed, but one does not have to be a prophet to know that the issue of assisted suicide will not go away. In a country that takes rights as seriously as we do, at some time the question will return to the courts, and it will enter through the door that the Supreme Court has left ajar.

1906 First euthanasia bill drafted in Ohio

1938 Euthanasia Society of America founded

1957 Lael Wertenbaker publishes *Death of a Man*

1967 Luis Kutner proposes living will

1969 Elisabeth Kübler-Ross publishes *On Death and Dying*

1973 Dr. Geertruide Postma stands trial in the Netherlands for helping her mother die; court finds her guilty, imposes light sentence, and lays down guidelines under which Dutch physicians may help patients die

1974 Euthanasia Society reborn as Society for the Right to Die

1976 New Jersey Supreme Court decides Karen Ann Quinlan case

1976 California Natural Death Act passed, first in nation to give legal standing to living wills and protect physicians from liability for not treating incurable illnesses

1980 Pope John Paul II issues declaration opposing mercy killing but approving greater use of painkillers to ease pain and the right to refuse extraordinary means for sustaining life

1980 Hemlock Society founded

1984 Rotterdam Court hands down criteria to guide physician-assisted dying

1984 Royal Dutch Medical Society announces approval of physician-assisted dying and sets out "Rules of Careful Conduct"

1988 *Journal of American Medical Association* prints "It's Over, Debbie"

1988 Roper Poll shows 58 percent of Americans favor legalizing physician aid in dying

1990   Washington Initiative 119 is filed, first state voter referendum

1990   Remmelink Report finds Dutch doctors not abusing protocols for assisting patients to die

1990   American Medical Association adopts formal position that with informed consent, physician can withhold or withdraw treatment from a patient close to death and may also discontinue life support of patient in permanent coma

1990   Jack Kevorkian helps Janet Adkins commit suicide

1990   Supreme Court decides Nancy Cruzan case

1990   Murder charge against Kevorkian in Adkins's death dismissed

1990   Congress passes Patient Self-Determination Act

1991   Dr. Timothy Quill writes about helping "Diane" die

1991   Derek Humphry publishes *Final Exit*

1991   Washington State voters reject Initiative 119 by 54 to 46 margin

1992   California voters defeat Proposition 161, which would have allowed for physician-assisted suicide, by 54 to 46 margin

1993   Compassion in Dying founded in Washington State

1994   All fifty states and District of Columbia now recognize advance directives

1994   In *Compassion in Dying v. Washington,* federal district judge Barbara Rothstein overturns Washington State law prohibiting assisted suicide

1994   In *Quill v. Koppel,* federal district judge Thomas P. Griesa upholds New York State law criminalizing assisted suicide

1994   Dutch television carries broadcast of actual euthanasia

1994   Oregon voters, by 51 to 49 margin, approve Measure 16, allowing certain terminally ill patients to obtain prescriptions to end their lives

1995   Ninth Circuit Court of Appeals reverses lower court and upholds Washington State law against assisted suicide

1995   Second Dutch commission reaffirms finding of Remmelink report

1995   U.S. district judge Michael Hogan rules that Measure 16 violates Equal Protection Clause and suspends its implementation

1996   Ninth Circuit Court of Appeals, sitting *en banc,* reverses panel and strikes down Washington law on due process grounds; also reverses Judge Hogan on Measure 16

1996   Michigan jury acquits Kevorkian of violating new state law banning assisted suicide

1996   Second Circuit Court of Appeals strikes down New York State law against assisted suicide on equal protection grounds

1997   Supreme Court hears arguments in *Washington v. Glucksberg* and *Quill v. Vacco*

1997   Oregon legislature votes to return Measure 16 to voters for review

1997   U.S. Supreme Court hands down rulings in two cases, finding there is no constitutionally protected right to assisted suicide; five justices file concurring opinions

1997   Oregon voters approve Measure 16 again, this time by 60 to 40 margin

1998   First patient dies with assistance of physician under Measure 16

1998   Kevorkian administers lethal injection to Thomas Youk; videotape is then broadcast on *60 Minutes;* Kevorkian indicted for murder

1999   Kevorkian found guilty of second-degree murder; sentenced to 10–25 years in prison

Compassion in Dying v. Washington, 850 F. Supp. 1454 (W.D. Wash. 1994)

Compassion in Dying v. Washington, 49 F.3d 586 (9th Cir. 1995)

Compassion in Dying v. Washington, 79 F.3d 790 (9th Cir. 1996)

Cruzan v. Director, Missouri Department of Health, 497 U.S. 261 (1990)

Griswold v. Connecticut, 381 U.S. 479 (1965)

Lee v. Oregon, 891 F. Supp. 1421 (D. Ore. 1995)

Lee v. Oregon, 107 F.3d 1382 (9th Cir. 1997)

People v. Kevorkian, 527 N.W.2d 714 (Mich. 1994)

Planned Parenthood v. Casey, 505 U.S. 833 (1992)

Poe v. Ullman, 367 U.S. 497 (1961)

Quill v. Koppel, 870 F. Supp. 78 (S.D.N.Y. 1994)

Quill v. Vacco, 80 F.3d 716 (2d Cir. 1996)

Quinlan, In re, 355 A.2d 647 (N.J. 1976)

Roe v. Wade, 410 U.S. 113 (1973)

Satz v. Perlmutter, 379 So.2d 359 (Fla. 1980)

Vacco v. Quill, 117 S. Ct. 2293 (1997)

Washington v. Glucksberg, 117 S. Ct. 2258 (1997)

BIBLIOGRAPHICAL ESSAY

Note from the Series Editors: The following bibiliographical essay contains the primary and secondary sources the author consulted for this volume. We have asked all authors in the series to omit formal citations in order to make our volumes more readable, inexpensive, and appealing for students and general readers. In adopting this format, Landmark Law Cases and American Society follows the precedent of a number of highly regarded and widely consulted series.

The best single-volume introduction to the general topic of right to die is Peter G. Filene, *In the Arms of Others: A Cultural History of the Right-to-Die in America* (Chicago: Ivan R. Dee, 1998). For legal aspects of the right to die, see the authoritative Alan Meisel, *The Right to Die* (New York: John Wiley, 1989) and its subsequent updated supplements; a more popular study that goes through the Cruzan case is Melvin I. Urofsky, *Letting Go: Death, Dying and the Law* (New York: Scribner's, 1993).

While there is as yet no study of physician-assisted suicide that explores the social, cultural, and political as well as the medical and legal aspects, the following are useful: Ira Byock, *Dying Well: Peace and Possibilities at the End of Life* (New York: Riverhead Books, 1997); Ronald Dworkin, *Life's Dominion: An Argument About Abortion, Euthanasia and Individual Freedom* (New York: Knopf, 1993); Timothy Quill, *Death and Dignity: Making Choices and Taking Charge* (New York: Norton, 1993); Lonny Shavelson, *A Chosen Death: The Dying Confront Assisted Suicide* (New York: Simon & Schuster, 1995); James M. Hoefler and Brian E. Kamoie, *Deathright: Culture, Medicine, Politics and the Right to Die* (Boulder: Westview Press, 1994); and Jennifer M. Scherer and Rita J. Simon, *Euthanasia and the Right to Die: A Comparative View* (Lanham: Rowman & Littlefield, 1999). A good sampling of different viewpoints can be found in Tom L. Beauchamp, *Intending Death: The Ethics of Assisted Suicide and Euthanasia* (Upper Saddle River: Prentice Hall, 1996).

One of the earliest statements by a doctor is by the noted heart surgeon Christiaan Barnard, *Good Life Good Death: A Doctor's Case for Euthanasia and Suicide* (Englewood Cliffs: Prentice Hall, 1980). See also Milton Heifetz, *Easier Said Than Done: Moral Decisions in Medical Uncertainty* (Amherst: Prometheus Books, 1992). Most of the debate takes place in medical journals, and some of the more useful articles include Howard Brody, "Assisted Death: A Compassionate Response to a Medical Failure," 327 *New England Journal of Medicine* 1384 (1992), and "Causing, Intending and Assisting Death," 4 *Journal of Clinical Ethics* 112 (1993); N. S. Jecker, "Giving Death a Hand: When the Dying and the Doctor Stand in a Special Relationship," 39 *Journal of the American Geriatric Society* 831 (1995); Thomas A. Preston, "Professional Norms and Physician Attitudes toward Euthanasia," 22 *Journal of Law, Medicine and Ethics* 36 (1994); and Robert F. Weir, "The Morality of Physician-Assisted Suicide," 20 *Law, Medicine & Health Care* 116 (1992). The famous story about Dr. Quill and "Diane" is in Quill, "Death and Dignity: A Case of Individualized Decision-Making," 324 *New England Journal of Medicine* 691 (1994).

For suicide, see Margaret P. Battin, *Ethical Issues in Suicide* (Upper Saddle River: Prentice Hall, 1995), and *The Least Worst Death: Essays in Bioethics on the End of Life* (New York: Oxford University Press, 1994); George Burnell, *Final Choices: To Live or Die in an Age of Medical Technology* (New York: Insight Books, 1993); Donald W. Cox, *Hemlock's Cup* (Amherst: Prometheus Books, 1993); and Derek Humphry, *Let Me Die Before I Wake: How Dying People End Their Suffering* (Eugene: Hemlock Society, 1991). One should also see the many books available on bioethics, but start with Tom L. Beauchamp and James F. Childress, *Principles of Biomedical Ethics, 4th ed.* (New York: Oxford University Press, 1994), and Daniel Callahan, *The Troubled Dream of Life* (New York: Simon & Schuster, 1993).

For the Dutch experience, see Carlos F. Gomez, *Regulating Death: Euthanasia and the Case of the Netherlands* (New York: Free Press, 1991); Margaret Battin, "Voluntary Euthanasia and the Risks of Abuse: Can We Learn Anything from the Netherlands?" 20 *Law, Medicine & Health Care* 133 (1992); G. E. Pence, "Do Not Go Slowly into That Dark Night: Mercy Killing in Holland," 84 *American Journal of Medicine* 139 (1988); P. J. van der Maas, et al., "Euthanasia and Other Medical Decisions Concerning the End of Life," 338 *Lancet* 669 (1991); and Maurice A. M. de Wachter, "Euthanasia in the Netherlands," 22 *Hastings Center Report* 23 (1992).

Law reviews have carried a number of articles about right to die cases in general and have also started to look into the question of assisted suicide. One can begin with Cass R. Sunstein, "The Right to Die," 106 *Yale Law Journal* 1123 (1997); Yale Kamisar, "The Reasons So Many People Support Physician-Assisted Suicide—And Why These Reasons Are Not Convincing," 12 *Issues in Law & Medicine* 113 (1996); note "Physician-Assisted Suicide: State Legislation Teetering at the Pinnacle of a Slippery Slope," 7 *William & Mary Bill of Rights Journal* 277 (1998); Susan R. Martyn and Henry J. Bourguignon, "Physician-Assisted Suicide: The Lethal Flaws of the Ninth and Second Circuit Decisions," 85 *California Law Review* 371 (1997); and Robert M. Hardaway, Miranda K. Peterson, and Cassandra Mann, "The Right to Die and the Ninth Amendment: Compassion and Dying after *Glucksberg* and *Vacco*," 7 *George Mason Law Review* 313 (1999).

One of the most useful places for getting current information about assisted suicide, both pro and con, is the Internet. Nearly every group now has a web site, and merely listing them would take dozens of pages. The site *www.euthanasia.com* provides basic information as well as links to many other sites; *www.rights.org/deathnet* has citations to academic articles on the subject, as does *wings.buffalo.edu.faculty/research/bioethics/journal.html* (which also has links to related pages). Any good search engine will lead the student to numerous sites.

INDEX